PREFACE

1. Scope

This publication provides joint doctrine for the planning and execution of counterterrorism across the range of military operations.

2. Purpose

This publication has been prepared under the direction of the Chairman of the Joint Chiefs of Staff. It sets forth joint doctrine to govern the activities and performance of the Armed Forces of the United States in joint operations and provides the doctrinal basis for interagency coordination and for US military involvement in multinational operations. It provides military guidance for the exercise of authority by combatant commanders and other joint force commanders (JFCs) and prescribes joint doctrine for operations, education, and training. It provides military guidance for use by the Armed Forces in preparing their appropriate plans. It is not the intent of this publication to restrict the authority of the JFC from organizing the force and executing the mission in a manner the JFC deems most appropriate to ensure unity of effort in the accomplishment of the overall objective.

3. Application

a. Joint doctrine established in this publication applies to the Joint Staff, commanders of combatant commands, subunified commands, joint task forces, subordinate components of these commands, and the Services.

b. The guidance in this publication is authoritative; as such, this doctrine will be followed except when, in the judgment of the commander, exceptional circumstances dictate otherwise. If conflicts arise between the contents of this publication and the contents of Service publications, this publication will take precedence unless the Chairman of the Joint Chiefs of Staff, normally in coordination with the other members of the Joint Chiefs of Staff, has provided more current and specific guidance. Commanders of forces operating as part of a multinational (alliance or coalition) military command should follow multinational doctrine and procedures ratified by the United States. For doctrine and procedures not ratified by the United States, commanders should evaluate and follow the multinational command's doctrine and procedures, where applicable and consistent with US law, regulations, and doctrine.

For the Chairman of the Joint Chiefs of Staff:

LLOYD J. AUSTIN III
Lieutenant General, USA
Director, Joint Staff

Intentionally Blank

TABLE OF CONTENTS

CHAPTER V

SIGNIFICANT ENABLING FUNCTIONS FOR COUNTERTERRORISM

APPENDIX

GLOSSARY

FIGURE

- **Provides joint doctrine for the planning and execution of counterterrorism (CT) across the range of military operations.**

- **Describes the strategic campaign framework for CT.**

- **Provides insight into terrorist behaviors, examines terrorist motivations, and provides observations of general terrorist characteristics.**

- **Presents prevalent models of terrorist organizations and terrorist approaches to planning and execution.**

- **Summarizes the relationship of CT to irregular warfare.**

- **Describes the direct and indirect operational approaches to CT.**

- **Outlines CT roles, responsibilities, and authorities – command and control.**

- **Discusses significant enabling functions for CT - intelligence; intelligence, surveillance, and reconnaissance; logistics; legal; strategic communication; and information operations.**

Overview

Terrorism had been treated primarily as a law enforcement issue by most countries and international organizations because it represents extreme lawlessness.

Terrorism has evolved as a preferred tactic for ideological extremists around the world, directly or indirectly affecting millions of people. In addition to increasing law enforcement capabilities for counterterrorism (CT), the United States (US), like many nations, developed specialized, but limited, military CT capabilities. In joint doctrine, CT was simply defined as operations that include the offensive measures taken to prevent, deter, preempt, and respond to terrorism.

The broader construct of combating terrorism is defined as "actions, including antiterrorism and counterterrorism (CT), taken to oppose terrorism throughout the entire threat spectrum."

In addition to any diplomatic and law enforcement actions, the US Government (USG) typically viewed CT missions as special operations by covert, clandestine, or low visibility means. CT is one of the core tasks of the US special operations forces (SOF), and their role and additive capability is to conduct offensive measures within Department of Defense's (DOD's) overall combating terrorism (CbT) efforts. Some significant policy and strategy adjustments were required because terrorism has evolved from a tactic of inducing fear in select populations/areas to a transnational threat of strategic proportion.

CT: "Actions taken directly against terrorist networks and indirectly to influence and render global and regional environments inhospitable to terrorist networks."

After September 11, 2001, the US, along with multinational partners, embarked on what was characterized as a "global war on terrorism (GWOT)." That war has proven the need for expanded CT capabilities and a broader role for the US military in unified action against terrorism. That increasing role for conventional forces (CF), the need for truly unified action, and an increased emphasis on an indirect approach has led to developing this doctrine with a new definition for CT.

The United States Government (USG) policy on countering terrorism has been summarized as follows: Defeat violent extremism, and create a global environment that is inhospitable to violent extremists.

The Department of State (DOS) was given the lead in developing policy action plans that employ both incentives and disincentives to end state sponsorship of terrorism.

Unity of effort requires coordination not only at the apex of the federal government but also at the operational/tactical level, where response and intervention actions may be taken by diverse authorities acting independently or in coordination with each other. This policy requires what is doctrinally known as unified action, also called the "whole of government approach" by many interagency partners.

National Strategy.

The broad USG strategy is to continue to lead an international effort to deny violent extremist networks the resources and functions they need to operate and survive. This strategy of three key elements and three enabling elements represents the critical efforts (the ways) for achieving success. **The key strategy elements are**: protect and defend the homeland; attack terrorists and their capacity to operate effectively at home and abroad; and support mainstream efforts to reject violent extremism. The three key elements of the strategy are enabled by three crosscutting elements: expanding foreign partnerships and partnership capacity; enhancing capacity to prevent terrorist acquisition and use of weapons of mass destruction (WMD); and institutionalizing, domestically and internationally, the strategy against violent extremists.

Department of Defense Strategy for Combating Terrorism.

The **DOD strategy for CbT** is derived from the *National Security Strategy* and implements the *National Strategy for Combating Terrorism*. **Objectives** are summarized as follows: thwart or defeat terrorist attacks against the US, our partner nations (PNs), and interests; attack and disrupt terrorist networks abroad so as to cause adversaries to be incapable or unwilling to attack the US homeland, allies, or interests; deny terrorist networks WMD; establish conditions that allow PNs to govern their territory effectively and defeat terrorists; and deny a hospitable environment to violent extremists.

Military Strategic Approach.

The **military strategic approach** is to focus military operations in such a way as to assist the other instruments of national power to undermine the terrorists' center of gravity: extremist ideology. The Armed Forces of the United States will pursue direct and indirect approaches to counter the terrorists' ideology, support moderate alternatives, build rapport with and capacities of partners, and attack the terrorist and their infrastructure.

Military Strategic Objectives.

The **military strategic objectives** provide a way to achieve the national strategic aims (end state). They are:

Deny terrorists the resources they need to operate and survive.

Enable partner nations to counter terrorism. Prevent WMD proliferation, recover and eliminate uncontrolled materials, and maintain capacity for consequence management.

Defeat terrorists and their organizations.

Counter state and non-state support for terrorism in coordination with other government agencies (OGAs) and PNs.

Contribute to the establishment of conditions that counter ideological support for terrorism.

Prioritized Strategic End States for the Global War on Terrorism.

Planning starts with the overarching *National Defense Strategy* from which the *Guidance for Employment of the Force* (GEF) derives prioritized regional and functional strategic end states. The **functional end states for the GWOT** in the GEF are:

End State 1. Organizations committed to violent extremism no longer have the capability or intent to strike globally and catastrophically and their capacity to strike is outweighed by the capacity of local governments to counter and defeat them.

End State 2. Key states deny the enemy the resources needed to operate and survive. In particular, key states have reduced ungoverned or under governed areas that violent extremists seek to exploit.

End State 3. Terrorists, violent extremists, and their supporters are prevented from obtaining, developing, distributing, or using WMD.

End State 4. The global environment is inhospitable to terrorism and violent extremism.

Irregular Warfare (IW).

Irregular warfare (IW) is a violent struggle among state and non-state actors for legitimacy and influence over the relevant populations. IW favors indirect approaches and asymmetric means, though it may involve the full range of military and other capabilities, in order to erode an adversary's power, influence, and will.

IW involves a variety of operations and activities that occur in isolation or combined with conventional force operations.

CT is an activity of IW. An adversary using irregular methods typically will endeavor to wage protracted operations in an attempt to break the will of their opponent and influence relevant populations. Activities applicable to IW include, but are not limited to: foreign internal defense, security force assistance, counterinsurgency (COIN), CT, unconventional warfare, stability operations, strategic communication (SC), psychological operations, information operations (IO), civil-military operations, intelligence and counterintelligence, and law enforcement.

The key to success in IW comes from the ability of a group or organization to influence populations to gain or enhance political authority.

The **focus of IW is on the relevant population and not military platforms or armed forces,** as it is in traditional war. IW is a struggle for legitimacy and influence over a population from which its authority to act originates, and is conferred upon either its government or leadership. IW depends not just on military prowess, but also an understanding of such social dynamics as tribal politics, social networks, religious influences, and cultural mores. CT efforts should include all instruments of national power to undermine an adversary's power and will, and its credibility and legitimacy to influence the relevant population.

Terrorist Threats

America is at war with

Violent extremists find it useful to mischaracterize the war *extremists who advocate and use violence to gain control over others and threaten our way of life.*

as a religious or cultural clash. These violent extremists see the US and other Western societies as primary obstacles to achieving their political ends. The greatest strength of our society is its freedom and openness. The extremist networks will continue to exploit the seams in open societies around the globe, and consequently, the US and PNs remain vulnerable to terrorist violence designed to undermine those relationships and cause some members to abandon the struggle.

Terrorist networks, such as al-Qaeda, may employ irregular, catastrophic, or disruptive methods to challenge United States (US) security interests.

Irregular threats involve the employment of "unconventional" methods and tactics to counter the traditional advantages of stronger opponents. Catastrophic threats involve the acquisition, possession, and potential use of WMD or methods and material producing WMD-like effects. Disruptive threats may come from terrorist organizations that develop and use breakthrough technologies to negate current US advantages.

Nature of the Enemy.

Terrorist groups, regardless of ideology, origin, location, or organizational structure have some common basic needs to survive and remain credible to their followers: funding, security, an ability to produce and distribute propaganda, a support infrastructure, an ability to recruit, and the means to conduct violent acts against selected targets. **The principal enemy is a transnational movement, consisting of extremist organizations, networks, and individuals – and their state and non-state supporters – which uses terrorism for ideological ends.** Our secondary enemy is the other collective violent extremist organizations (VEOs) that interfere with our CT efforts and which may transition to overt sponsorship of or active participation in direct action against the US, our PNs, and our interests.

There are a variety of state and non-state actors identified with terrorism that have been generally categorized as opportunists, extremists, and terrorists.

Opportunists are members of criminal organizations (e.g., narcoterrorists), weapon proliferators, or state sponsors, who undercut the rule of law and governmental legitimacy, contributing to an environment of corruption and violence.

Extremists are those who seek to force their ideological beliefs on others. They oppose - in principle and practice - the right of people to choose how to live and how to organize their societies; and support the murder of ordinary people to advance their extremist ideological objectives.

Terrorist refers to those who commit acts of terrorism.

Terrorist Behavior.

Terrorism is a tactic selected after rational consideration of the costs and benefits in order to achieve an objective.

Terrorism is a rationally selected tactic usually employed in the pursuit of ideological aims. However, some individuals or small violent organizations that employ terrorist means may not always be concerned with particular causes or an avowed ideology. These terrorists may be motivated purely by a desire to commit violent acts.

Some terrorists have utopian goals regardless of their aims. This utopianism expresses itself forcefully as an extreme degree of impatience with the "status quo" of the rest of the world that validates the terrorists' extreme methods. Change, and the destructive method by which change is brought about, may be much more important than the end result.

Terrorists within groups usually have different behaviors collectively than individually. Groups are collectively more daring and ruthless than the individual members. The individual terrorist does not want to appear less committed than the others, and will not object to proposals within the group that they would not consider as an individual.

Understanding and knowledge of a violent extremist organization's preferences and capabilities provides a baseline to conduct successful CT operations and promotes the use of active approaches, both direct and indirect, to counter the threat.

Strategies against terrorists require understanding their point of view.

Terrorist groups require recruitment, preparation, and integration into the operational structure of the group. A group's leadership will not employ assets without weighing the value of the asset, the probability of success, and the potential benefits to the group.

Terrorist strategies are aimed at publicly causing damage to symbols or inspiring fear. Timing, location, and method of attacks accommodate media dissemination and ensure wide-spread reporting to maximize impact. In its purest form, a terrorist operation often will have the goal of manipulating popular perceptions, and strives to achieve this by controlling or dictating media coverage.

Ideology and motivation are the primary characteristics that influence the objectives of terrorist operations. Groups with secular ideologies and nonreligious goals often will attempt highly selective and discriminate acts of violence to achieve a specific political aim.

Terrorist Characteristics.

In general, terrorists often feel alienated from society, have a perceived grievance, or regard themselves as victims of an injustice. Terrorists most commonly originate from middle class backgrounds, with some coming from extreme wealth and privilege. In general, terrorists, especially their leaders, are usually of average or better intelligence and have been exposed to advanced education. Terrorist groups increasingly are recruiting members with expertise in areas such as communications, computer programming, engineering, finance, and the sciences. Terrorists are often unremarkable in individual characteristics and attempts to "profile" likely terrorist groups' members may not be productive.

A terrorist organization is characterized by its levels of commitment, the tactical level cellular organization, group organizational structure, and its primary motivation.

Typically, there are **four different levels of commitment** within a terrorist organization: passive supporters, active supporters, cadre, and leadership. **Leaders** provide direction and policy; approve goals and objectives; and provide overarching guidance for operations. **Cadre** is the nucleus of "active" members, the zealots, who comprise the core of a terrorist organization. This echelon plans and conducts not only operations, but also manages areas of intelligence, finance, logistics, IO, and communications. **Active supporters** participate in the political, fund-raising, and information activities of the group. Usually, they are fully aware of their relationship to the terrorist group but do not commit violent acts. **Passive supporters** are typically individuals or groups that are sympathetic to the announced goals and intentions of the terrorist organization or its ideology, but are not committed enough to take action.

Tactical-level Cellular Organization.

One of the primary reasons for a cellular or compartmental structure is security.

The smallest elements of terrorist organizations are the cells at the tactical level — the building blocks for the terrorist organization. A cellular structure makes it difficult for an adversary to penetrate the entire organization, and the compromise or loss of one cell does not compromise the identity, location, or actions of other cells. Personnel within one cell may not be aware of the existence of other cells or their personnel and, therefore, cannot divulge sensitive information to infiltrators or captors.

Group Organizational Structure.

There are **two typical organizational structures** used by terrorist groups: **networked and hierarchical**

Hierarchical Structure.

Hierarchical structure organizations have a well-defined vertical chain of command and responsibility. Information flows up and down organizational channels that correspond to these vertical chains, but may not move horizontally. This is more traditional, and is common of groups that are well established with a command and support structure. Normally, only the cell leader has knowledge of other cells or contacts, and only senior leadership has visibility of the entire organization.

Networked Structure.

A **network structure** may be a variation of several basic nodal concepts, a node being an individual, a cell, another networked organization, or even a hierarchical organization. A terrorist network may consist of parts of other organizations (even governments), which are acting in ways that can be exploited to achieve the network's organizational goals. There are **three basic types of network structures**, depending on the ways in which elements (nodes) are linked to other elements of the structure: the chain, hub (or star and wheel), and all-channel. In a **chain** type structure each node links to the node next in sequence and communication between the nodes is by passing information along the line. In the **hub (or star and wheel)** type structure outer nodes communicate with one central node, which may not be the leader or decision maker for the network. In the **all-channel** type structure all nodes are connected to each other. The network is organizationally "flat," meaning there is no hierarchical command structure above it. Command and control is distributed within the network.

A terrorist group may also employ a hybrid structure that combines elements of more than one network type.

Categories of Terrorist Organizations.

There are many different categories of terrorism and terrorist groups. These categories serve to differentiate terrorist organizations according to specific criteria, which are usually related to the field or specialty of whoever is selecting the categories.

Government Affiliation Categories.

Categorizing terrorist groups by their affiliation with governments provides indications of their means for intelligence, operations, and access to types of weapons.

Motivation Categories.	Motivation categories describe terrorist groups in terms of their ultimate goals or objectives. While political or religious ideologies will determine the "how" of the conflict, and the sort of society that will arise from a successful conclusion, motivation is the "what" in terms of end state or measure of success.
Ideological Categories.	Ideological categories describe the political, religious, or social orientation of the group. While some groups will be seriously committed to their avowed ideologies, for others, ideology is poorly understood, and primarily a justification for their actions to outsiders or sympathizers
Proliferation of Knowledge Between Organizations.	Terrorist groups increase their capabilities through the exchange of knowledge. Military professionals must evaluate potential terrorist threats according to what capabilities they may acquire through known or suspected associations with other groups, or those capabilities that can be acquired through the study and employment of techniques and approaches that have proven successful for other terrorist organizations.
Terrorist Approaches.	**Terrorist operations typically are planned in great detail with the objectives of minimizing risk, achieving the highest probability of success, and attaining the widest publicity of their actions.** Terrorists seek to avoid adversary strengths and concentrate on their weaknesses. Terrorist tactics are aligned with their overall plans which attempt to use the successful achievement of their operational objectives to realize the accomplishment of their strategic goals.
Terrorist Approach to Planning and Execution. *Exploitation is the primary objective of all terrorist operations.*	Terrorist operational planning can be analyzed according to requirements common to all operations. The planning and operation cycle of broad target selection, intelligence gathering and surveillance, specific target selection, pre-attack surveillance and planning, rehearsals, actions on the objective, and escape and exploitation is valid for traditional hierarchically organized groups, as well as decentralized "network" type organizations.
Terrorist Approach to Operations and Tactics.	The combination of methods and approaches is virtually unlimited. **Common themes in terrorist operations are surprise, secrecy, innovation, and indirect methods of attack.** Terrorist operations are unique, in that each is planned for a specific target and effect.

Forms of Terrorist Tactics. Terrorist tactics take many forms. Some are accomplished as independent actions. Others may be undertaken as part of other coordinated activities. **The more common types of terrorist tactics are**: threat or hoax; arson; sabotage; bombing; kidnapping; hostage taking; hijacking; raid or ambush; seizure; assassination; and weapons of mass destruction.

Terrorist Information Operations and Public Relations Activities. **The Internet provides terrorists and extremists the means** to spread their radical ideology, an ad hoc means of operational connectivity, and a link to the full-media spectrum for public relations. The Internet facilitates their recruiting, training, logistic support, planning, fundraising, etc. The internet is also a powerful tool to conduct the equivalent of media facilitated IO against the US and PNs.

Operational Approaches

IW, and especially the employment of terrorist tactics, has become the "warfare of choice" for some state and non-state adversaries. US superiority in conventional warfighting drives many of our adversaries to avoid direct military confrontation with the US. They employ a strategy of physical, economic, and psychological subversion and attrition to undermine, erode, and ultimately exhaust the national power, influence, and will of the US and its strategic partners.

The strategic campaign framework for CT is composed of three elements: friendly, enemy, and the global environment. **The structure of the campaign uses five logical lines of operations (LOOs)** further divided into two categories consisting of efforts applied directly against the enemy and actions applied indirectly to influence the global environment. These are referred to as direct and indirect approaches. The aims of the strategic campaign are to create a stabilized global environment which is inhospitable to terrorists and their organizations, and to isolate, defeat, and prevent the reemergence of a terrorist threat.

Integrated Approaches. **The campaign plan for the war on terrorism makes use of both direct and indirect approaches.** Either or both approaches may be conducted within the scope of a broader campaign as directed by a joint force commander (JFC). The ability to manage both approaches to harness their synergistic effects is vital to the success of both near- and long-term CT objectives.

Direct Approach.

The **direct approach** describes actions taken against terrorists and terrorist organizations. The goals of the direct approach against terrorists and their organizations are to defeat a specific threat through neutralization/dismantlement of the network (including actors, resources, and support structures) and to prevent the reemergence of a threat once neutralized.

Indirect Approach.

The **indirect approach** describes the means by which the global combating terrorism network (GCTN) can influence the operational environments within which CT campaigns/operations are conducted. This approach usually includes actions taken within LOOs to enable partners to conduct operations against terrorists and their organizations as well as actions taken to shape and stabilize those environments as a means to erode the capabilities of terrorist organizations and degrade their ability to acquire support and sanctuary.

Terrorist Model.

To understand the nature of the development of VEOs, the war on terrorism campaign plan uses a circular model that represents the four critical enabling components in the cycle of terrorist operations that facilitates development of a global terrorism network. The components are: a *populace* from which extremists have the potential to draw support; the *tacit and/or active support* given to the extremist by some of the sympathetic populace; *local/regional terrorism* as a result of states unwilling or incapable of countering violent extremists; and *global terrorism* that results from global networks built upon popular support and the inability of states to control local and regional extremist networks.

Counterterrorism Model.

The CT model is a model based on the application of the indirect and direct approach LOOs from the strategic campaign framework against the circular model of the terrorism threats. This model addresses each of the critical components of the threat circle with five lines of operation from the direct and indirect approaches - erode support for extremist ideology; enable partners to combat VEOs; deter tacit and active support for VEOs; disrupt VEOs; and deny access and/or use of WMD by VEOs. The desired objectives of these LOOs are to: defeat the VEOs; isolate the VEOs: prevent reconstitution/emergence of VEOs, defend the homeland against VEOs.

Conventional forces and special operations forces each possess unique capabilities that can produce even greater warfighting potential for the joint force commanders (JFCs) when integrated into a holistic global CT campaign with numerous theater CT operations.

CT is a core task of SOF, but global demand for CT activities and the varied conditions under which the broad range of CT activities occur dictates that SOF cannot be the sole force engaged in CT operations. Executing protracted **CT operations will increasingly require CF** to perform missions that traditionally have been viewed primarily as SOF activities. Circumstances may dictate that SOF support CF; and conversely, that CF support SOF.

Command and Control

Effectively countering terrorism may require more complex command and control and interagency coordination.

Rarely in history have the effects of tactical level actions been so pronounced at the national strategic level as during the large scale CT and COIN operations in Iraq and Afghanistan. This realization has been fully recognized by the national level authorities and down the chain of command to the warfighters.

President and Secretary of Defense.

When the President directs that CT operations be conducted, the Armed Forces of the United States provide the military instrument of national power. Secretary of Defense (SecDef) is responsible to the President for creating, supporting, and employing military capabilities, to include CT military capabilities.

National Security Council.

The National Security Council is the principal forum for consideration of national security policy requiring Presidential determination. Of high importance among these policy determinations are the national security implications of terrorism and CT.

National Counterterrorism Center.

The National Counterterrorism Center (NCTC) is the primary organization in the USG for integrating and analyzing all intelligence possessed or acquired pertaining to terrorism (except purely domestic terrorism). It provides all-source intelligence support to government-wide CT activities; establishes its own information technology systems and architectures, and those between the NCTC and other agencies. The NCTC serves as the principal advisor to the Director of National Intelligence (DNI) on intelligence operations and analysis relating to CT. **Unique among US agencies, the NCTC also serves as the primary organization for strategic operation planning for CT.** It is responsible for the integration of all instruments of national power to the CT mission.

Commander, US Special Operations Command.

Commander, US Special Operations Command (CDRUSSOCOM) is responsible for synchronizing planning for global operations against terrorist networks, and will do so in coordination with other combatant commands, the Services, and, as directed, appropriate USG agencies.

Geographic Combatant Commanders (GCCs).

For global operations against terrorist networks, typically a geographic combatant commander (GCC) is the supported combatant commander (CCDR) with the CDRUSSOCOM supporting. However, for specific missions as may be directed by the President or SecDef, CDRUSSOCOM may be the supported CCDR with the GCC(s) supporting in their area(s) of responsibility (AOR)(s). To provide the necessary unity of command, **GCCs are normally authorized a theater special operations command (TSOC)** — a subunified command which serves as the primary organization by which the GCC exercises command and control (C2) over SOF. The TSOC also serves as a joint force special operations component command equivalent to a Service component command under the GCC.

The GCCs have the best regional focus and knowledge of the operational environment in their areas of responsibility.

Joint Task Force.

The C2 requirements for a joint task force (JTF) for CT operations are largely dependent upon its size, composition, organization, mission, the situation, and the size of the joint operations area. CT operations may be part of a larger IW-type situation (e.g., insurgency) for which the JFC is responsible. The GCC will designate a subordinate JFC and establish the JTF on a functional or geographic basis. When integrating CF and SOF for joint operations, the JFC will typically establish support relationships, often with mission-type orders, or alternatively, some operations may require tactical control as the command relationship.

Multinational CT command structures follow the same premise as for other multinational operations.

In working with multinational partners, the success of CT operations hinges on the US ability to work within each partner's political restraints, traditional structures, policies, and procedures. This requirement includes a multinational partner's willingness to not only coordinate and operate with the US military but with OGAs as well.

Interagency Coordination.

Success in the war against terrorism requires interagency

coordination to maximize the effectiveness of all instruments of national power. US Special Operations Command (USSOCOM), as the integrating command for global CT planning efforts, supports a growing network of relationships through continuous liaison partnerships, a supporting technical infrastructure, and using information sharing policies.

Joint Interagency Coordination Groups.

To enhance interagency coordination at the strategic and operational levels, **joint interagency coordination groups (JIACGs)** have been established at the GCCs. A CT planning effort and subsequent operations may require a combatant command to request additional CT expertise from various agencies and organizations to staff its JIACG and optimize interagency effectiveness and efficiency.

US Special Operations Command Interagency Task Force.

USSOCOM Interagency Task Force is a dedicated operations and intelligence planning team comprised of interagency intelligence and operations planning specialists and a robust information collection capability. The interagency task force searches for and identifies new, developing, and emerging CT opportunities to attack terrorist organizations and networks worldwide. It further develops actionable intelligence into operational courses of action and plans against the emerging targets. Combatant commands' JIACGs should coordinate their CT planning with the USSOCOM interagency task force as appropriate.

Significant Enabling Functions for Counterterrorism

Enabling functions requiring special emphasis for CT.

There are enabling functions that are essential to all joint operations, but require special emphasis for CT operations. These **significant enabling functions for CT are: intelligence; intelligence, surveillance, and reconnaissance (ISR); logistics; legal; SC; and IO.**

In the aftermath of the September 11, 2001 terrorist attacks, the USG enhanced CT intelligence architecture and interagency collaboration by setting clear national priorities and transforming the organizational structure of

The intelligence community (IC) has been reorganized and the DNI now oversees the IC to better integrate its efforts into a more unified, coordinated, and effective body. The President established a mission manager organization, the NCTC, dedicated solely to planning and conducting intelligence operations against terrorist networks.

The USSOCOM Center for Special Operations is the fusion point for DOD synchronization of CT plans and

the intelligence agencies to achieve those priorities.

establishing intelligence priorities against terrorist networks. Accurate and timely intelligence is absolutely critical to CbT. All disciplines of intelligence are required for CT.

Combatant commands require actionable intelligence, and that requirement is very relevant for CT operations from the strategic to the lowest tactical levels.

Intelligence requirements for global and regional operations against the primary enemy, the transnational terrorists (i.e., al-Qaeda), must also be synchronized with the intelligence requirements for regional operations (i.e., within AORs) against the secondary enemy, VEOs. GCCs have responsibility for intelligence analysis and production on all terrorist groups whose primary operating bases reside within their theater.

The responsible JFC must properly prioritize intelligence, surveillance, and reconnaissance for CT among other operational needs.

USSOCOM, the GCCs, Defense Intelligence Operations Coordination Center, DNI, and Joint Functional Component Command for Intelligence, Surveillance, and Reconnaissance coordinate and synchronize the ISR requirements and assets available to support the long war on terrorism. At the strategic and operational levels, the JFC employs ISR forces assigned or attached to the joint force and requests support of national/interagency assets through a validation by the supported CCDR, normally a GCC.

Logistic Planning.

The war against terrorism requires robust logistic planning with global distribution requirements for the Services. CT operations may receive priority over existing operations, and the transnational terrorist threat can require multiple CT operations within and across AORs. The numerous CT operations around the globe, utilizing various elements of US and PN instruments of national power, require continuing assessment, and prioritization of actions/support.

Commanders at all levels ensure their forces operate in accordance with the "law of war," often called the "law of armed conflict."

With CT operations in numerous locations across the globe, JFCs must be particularly aware of the status of their conflict, the legal basis for their use of force, the characterization of enemy combatants, civilians taking a direct part in the hostilities, and potential detainees. **The JFC responsible for CT should determine early in the planning stage what the required standing rules of engagement/standing rules for the use of force (ROE/RUF) should be.** When conducting multinational CT operations, the use of military force may be influenced by the differences between US and a host nation's and/or a PN's ROE/RUF.

Domestic CT operations are considered part of homeland security under the lead of Department of Homeland Security.

Department of Homeland Security is considered primary for coordinating Executive Branch efforts to detect, prepare for, prevent, protect against, respond to, and recover from terrorist attacks within the US. **In domestic situations, the Constitution, law, and DOD policy limit the scope and nature of military actions.** The President has the authority to direct the use of the military against terrorist groups and individuals in the US for other than law enforcement actions (i.e., national defense, emergency protection of life and property, and to restore order).

Effective use of strategic communication (SC) also can be used to counter violent extremist organizations' use of their own form of SC: ideological propaganda and disinformation.

The DOD SC objectives in the war on terrorism are to strengthen the GCTN by supporting PNs, converting moderates to become PNs, weaken sympathy and support for VEOs, provide support for moderate voices, dissuade enablers and supporters of extremists, counter ideological support for terrorism, and deter and disrupt terrorist acts. Subordinate JFCs must coordinate their SC activities with the CCDR to ensure they are consistent with USG objectives. GCCs must collaborate with the DOS diplomatic missions within their AORs.

CT is a mission area that focuses on effects of operations on people, and in some operational areas the "information war" can determine which side will gain the upper hand in public opinion.

IO are used to create and/or sustain desired and measurable effects on adversary leaders, forces (regular or irregular), information, information systems, and other audiences; while protecting and defending the JFC's own forces actions, information, and information systems. It is obvious that IO can and should be applied across the breadth and depth of CT operations as a primary means of influencing not only extremists and their supporters, but just as important, the moderates (mainstream populace). In CT operations, a goal is to identify the target audiences (TAs) and use IO to influence the TAs' behavior.

CONCLUSION

This publication provides joint doctrine for the planning and execution of counterterrorism across the range of military operations.

CHAPTER I
OVERVIEW

> *". . . We will not apologize for our way of life, nor will we waver in its defense, and for those who seek to advance their aims by inducing terror and slaughtering innocents, we say to you now that our spirit is stronger and cannot be broken; you cannot outlast us, and we will defeat you. . . ."*
>
> **President Barack Obama**
> **Inauguration Address, 20 January 2009**

1. General

Over several decades, terrorism has evolved as a preferred tactic for ideological extremists around the world, directly or indirectly affecting millions of people. Terrorism had been treated primarily as a law enforcement issue by most countries and international organizations because it represents extreme lawlessness. As the terrorist threat grew, in addition to increasing law enforcement capabilities for counterterrorism (CT), the United States, like many nations, developed specialized, but limited, military CT capabilities to rescue hostages, take preemptive action or retaliate against some terrorists because they were geographically or politically beyond the reach of law enforcement. In joint doctrine, CT was simply defined as operations that include the offensive measures taken to prevent, deter, preempt, and respond to terrorism. In addition to any diplomatic and law enforcement actions, the US Government (USG) typically viewed CT missions as special operations by covert, clandestine, or low visibility means. CT became one of the core tasks of the US special operations forces (SOF), and their role and additive capability is to conduct offensive measures within Department of Defense's (DOD's) overall combating terrorism (CbT) efforts.

a. The broader construct of CbT is defined as "actions, including antiterrorism and counterterrorism, taken to oppose terrorism throughout the entire threat spectrum." The early terrorist threat was generally from secular and nationalist terrorist groups, many of which depended upon active state sponsors. The collapse of the Soviet Union—which provided critical backing to terrorist groups and certain state sponsors—accelerated the decline in state sponsorship, and many terrorist organizations were effectively destroyed or neutralized, but that decline was short lived. Today, whether the extremists are local insurgents, participants in organized criminal activities, or members of an international terrorist network, if they use terrorist tactics, they are generally viewed as terrorists. Also, with the continued proliferation of weapons of mass destruction (WMD), the opportunity for terrorists to acquire and use them becomes more likely. Therefore, some significant policy and strategy adjustments were required because **terrorism has evolved from a tactic of inducing fear in select populations/areas to a transnational threat of strategic proportion,** particularly against the United States and Western societies. For example, Al-Qaeda and associated terrorist networks form a multinational enterprise with activities in more than 60 countries.

b. After September 11, 2001, the United States, along with multinational partners, embarked on what was characterized as a "global war on terrorism (GWOT)." That war has proven the need for expanded CT capabilities and a broader role for the US military in unified action against terrorism. DOD realized the size and scope of this global CT effort were beyond the capabilities of the CT dedicated SOF. While conventional forces (CF) continue to directly support some SOF CT operations, the pervasiveness of the threat has required that conventional forces also conduct CT operations. The 2006 *Quadrennial Defense Review Irregular Warfare Execution Roadmap* states, "the Military Departments and Services must continue to rebalance the capabilities and capacity to increase substantially their ability to conduct long-duration COIN [counterinsurgency] and CT operations, including operations with host nation security forces." **That increasing role for CF, the need for truly unified action, and an increased emphasis on an indirect approach has led to developing this doctrine with a new definition for CT:** "Actions taken directly against terrorist networks and indirectly to influence and render global and regional environments inhospitable to terrorist networks."

NATIONAL MILITARY STRATEGIC PLAN FOR THE WAR ON TERRORISM (1 FEBRUARY 2006)

The *National Military Strategic Plan for the War on Terrorism* (NMSP-WOT) was developed to address the specific need for focusing US military planning efforts to countering terrorism. The NMSP-WOT fulfilled the need for strategy and planning guidance and articulated the military contribution to achieving the objectives for the global war on terrorism identified in the *National Security Strategy, the National Defense Strategy, the National Military Strategy, and the National Strategy for Combating Terrorism.*

The NMSP-WOT was "operationalized" by the US Special Operations Command Concept Plan 7500, *Department of Defense Global War on Terrorism Campaign Plan.*

As a planning and source document, the NMSP-WOT was superseded by the 2008 *Joint Strategic Capabilities Plan* (JSCP), but much of the content of the NMSP-WOT remains relevant. The strategy and planning guidance that was consolidated in the superseded NMSP-WOT is now maintained within the functional planning guidance of the *Guidance for Employment of the Force* (GEF) while the more specific planning tasks are in the JSCP. The GEF moved the Department of Defense from a "contingency-centric" approach to planning to a "strategy-centric" approach. The GEF and JSCP are the "principal sources of guidance for combatant command steady-state campaign, contingency, and posture planning efforts.

Various Sources

---

c. This chapter **outlines the policies and strategies that influenced the development of the strategic campaign framework for CT doctrine.** The following paragraphs briefly introduce the national and DOD policies and strategies that led to and became part of the *National Military Strategic Plan for the War on Terrorism* (1 February 2006) (NMSP-WOT), which led to the development of the US Special Operations Command Concept Plan 7500, *Department of Defense Global War on Terrorism Campaign Plan.* While the 2008 *Joint Strategic Capabilities Plan* (JSCP) superseded the NMSP-WOT, some of its content was adopted into the JSCP and the *Guidance for Employment of the Force* (GEF), and now those documents are the principal sources for military strategy and planning guidance (including that for the GWOT). The **military strategic approach** and the **military strategic objectives,** are briefly discussed because of their historical relevance to the current framework for CT discussed in Chapter III, "Operational Approaches." That brief summary is followed by the prioritized strategic end states for the GWOT listed in the GEF. Then, the relationship of CT to irregular warfare (IW) is summarized, and the depth of the doctrinal foundation already associated with CT is explained.

2. **United States Government Policy and Strategy**

a. **Policy.** The *National Security Strategy* states, "It is the policy of the United States to seek and support democratic movements and institutions in every nation and culture, with the ultimate goal of ending tyranny in our world. In the world today, the fundamental character of regimes matters as much as the distribution of power among them. The goal of our statecraft is to help create a world of democratic, well-governed states that can meet the needs of their citizens and conduct themselves responsibly in the international system. This is the best way to provide enduring security for the American people." In conjunction with that broad policy, the USG policy on countering terrorism has been summarized as follows: **Defeat violent extremism, and create a global environment that is inhospitable to violent extremists.**

(1) In 2003, the *National Strategy for Combating Terrorism* listed a number of policy goals intended to establish and maintain an international standard of accountability with regard to CbT. They include:

(a) **A "zero tolerance" policy for terrorist activity.**

(b) Strong support for new, strict standards for all states to meet in the global war against terrorism.

(c) **States that have sovereign rights also have sovereign responsibilities.**

(d) The clear articulation of policy goals through appropriate public and diplomatic channels.

(2) To ensure the United States has a well orchestrated and synchronized policy, **the Department of State (DOS) was given the lead in developing policy action plans that employ both incentives and disincentives to end state sponsorship of terrorism.**

All appropriate USG departments and agencies were tasked to engage key allies to develop common or complementary strategies to support the policy action plans.

(3) Because each case is unique, with different interests and legacy issues involved **the USG does not have a single, inflexible approach to handling the recognized state sponsors of terrorism**. Each case is unique, with different interests and legacy issues involved. Each situation demands specifically tailored policies. The USG is open to overtures from states that want to put their sponsorship of terrorism behind them, but **remains resolute on the essential principle that there are no "good" or "just" terrorists.** The United States will be relentless in discrediting terrorism as a means of expressing discontent.

(4) An example of diplomacy supported by the USG policy is United Nations Security Council Resolution (UNSCR) 1373, which clearly established states' obligations for CbT. This resolution called upon all member states to cooperate to prevent terrorist attacks through a range of activities, including suppressing and freezing terrorist financing, prohibiting their nationals from financially supporting terrorists; denying safe havens to those who finance, plan, support, or commit terrorist acts; and taking steps to prevent the movement of terrorists. Additionally, the international CT conventions and protocols, together with UNSCR 1373, set forth a compelling body of international obligations relating to CT. The USG will continue to press all states to become parties to and fully implement these conventions and protocols.

(5) **Unity of effort requires coordination not only at the apex of the federal government but also at the operational/tactical level**, where response and intervention actions may be taken by diverse authorities acting independently or in coordination with each other. This policy requires what is doctrinally known as unified action, also called the "whole of government approach" by many interagency partners.

> *"An analysis of the history of combating terrorism confirms that the best way to defeat terrorism is to isolate and localize its activities and then destroy it through intensive, sustained action. This effort requires us to identify terrorists, locate their sanctuaries and destroy their ability to plan and operate."*
>
> **National Strategy for Combating Terrorism**
> **February 2003**

b. **National Strategy for Combating Terrorism.** Guidance for the war against extremism was derived from appropriate national security Presidential directives, the National Defense Strategy, contingency planning guidance, and the National Military Strategy. The consolidated guidance is summarized in the following national strategic aims, strategy, and means for the war on terrorism, and is depicted in Figure I-1. NOTE: Now, the GEF and the JSCP provide the principal planning guidance.

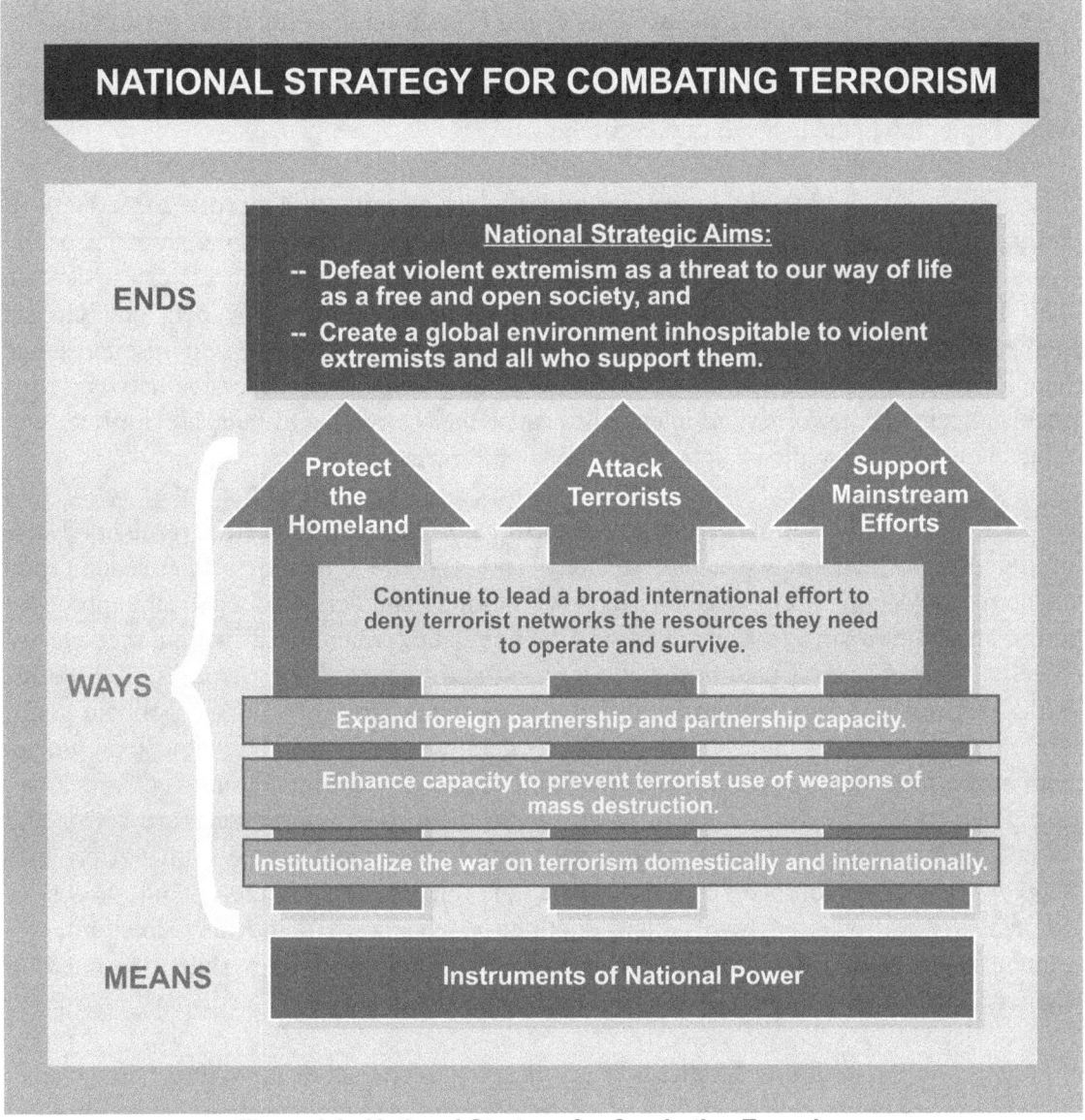

Figure I-1. National Strategy for Combating Terrorism

(1) **National Strategic Aims.** Defeat violent extremism as a threat to our way of life as a free and open society; and create a global environment inhospitable to violent extremists and all who support them (**the ends**).

(2) **National Strategy.**   The broad USG strategy is to continue to lead an international effort to deny violent extremist networks the resources and functions they need to operate and survive. This strategy of three key elements and three enabling elements represents the critical efforts **(the ways)** for achieving success.

(a) **Key Strategy Elements**

1. **Protect and Defend the Homeland.** These efforts protect and defend the economy, society, and systems of the USG from the effects of terrorist attacks. This element includes efforts both internal and external to the homeland because protecting and defending the homeland requires what can be characterized as a multilayered defense in depth beginning in the forward regions of the world.

2. **Attack Terrorists and their Capacity to Operate Effectively at Home and Abroad.** These direct offensive efforts are designed to disrupt terrorists' operations and can affect terrorists' ability to effectively execute their attacks or sustain their ideology. They include killing and capturing key terrorist leaders and tactical elements, destroying training centers, and denying the enemy access to resources and functions critical to their operations. Ultimately, continuous and successive network-wide attacks against the terrorists are intended to cause their networks to fail. USG efforts will typically need a transregional approach to counter terrorist networks.

3. **Support Mainstream Efforts to Reject Violent Extremism.** These efforts aim to counter extremist ideology and encourage democracy, freedom, and economic prosperity in societies. A decisive point in countering ideological support for terrorism occurs when a moderate group of the population, religious affiliation, sect, etc., of which the terrorists are a part, becomes active in the fight against the terrorists. Key to this is the moderates' belief that terrorism is not a legitimate means to pursue political goals. The strategy is to encourage and enable moderates to promote the view that violent extremist efforts undermine the wellbeing of the collective community on a local, regional, and global basis. A goal is for the mainstream moderates to become more active and successful in stopping support for the violent extremists. The US role in this effort is to support, where appropriate, and encourage and amplify the interests and voices of moderates who oppose extremists and continue to encourage democracy, freedom, and economic prosperity. **This is a key element of the national strategy that is focused on the terrorist's center of gravity (COG): extremist ideology.**

(b) **Enabling Elements.** The three key elements of the strategy are enabled by three crosscutting elements: expanding foreign partnerships and partnership capacity; enhancing capacity to prevent terrorist acquisition and use of WMD; and institutionalizing, domestically and internationally, the strategy against violent extremists.

(3) **Instruments of National Power.** Success in this war relies heavily on the close cooperation among USG and partner nations (PNs) to **integrate all instruments of their national power** — diplomatic, informational, military, and economic, and particularly the financial, intelligence, and law enforcement elements of those instruments (**the means**).

3. **Department of Defense Policy and Strategy**

a. **Policy.** DOD policy provides military commanders and their staffs with military objectives and relative priorities in the allocation of resources for CT. It also provides guidance for DOD cooperation with other USG departments and agencies and with PNs for planning and conducting CT operations. The resulting Department of Defense Global War on Terrorism Campaign Plan, and geographic combatant commanders' (GCCs') concept plans for the war on terrorism fulfill the DOD policy guidance.

b. **Department of Defense Strategy for Combating Terrorism.** The DOD strategy for CbT is derived from the *National Security Strategy* and implements the *National Strategy for Combating Terrorism.* Its objectives are summarized as follows:

(1) **Defeat Terrorist Attacks.** Thwart or defeat terrorist attacks against the United States, our PNs, and interests.

(2) **Attack Terrorist Networks Abroad.** Attack and disrupt terrorist networks abroad so as to cause adversaries to be incapable or unwilling to attack the US homeland, allies, or interests.

(3) **Deny Terrorist Networks WMD.** This includes possession or use of WMD.

(4) **Establish Favorable Conditions.** Establish conditions that allow PNs to govern their territory effectively and defeat terrorists.

(5) **Deny Hospitable Environment to Violent Extremists.** Contribute to the establishment and maintenance of a global environment inhospitable to violent extremist organizations (VEOs) and all who support them.

4. The Military Strategic Approach and Objectives for the War on Terrorism

The military strategic approach and military strategic objectives are summarized below because they are the basis for development of the strategic campaign framework for the Department of Defense Global War on Terrorism Campaign Plan and for the development of joint doctrine for CT. The principal military strategy and planning guidance are contained in the GEF and the JSCP.

a. **Military Strategic Approach.** The military strategic approach is to focus military operations in such a way as to assist the other instruments of national power to undermine the terrorists' COG: extremist ideology. The Armed Forces of the United States will pursue direct and indirect approaches to counter the terrorists' ideology, support moderate alternatives, build rapport with and capacities of partners, and attack the terrorist and their infrastructure. The direct approach focuses on protecting US interests while attacking the terrorists. The indirect approach focuses on the actions to establish conditions (a stable and more secure environment) for others to achieve success, and if necessary, with the help of the United States. Figure I-2 depicts the military strategic approach and provides the foundation for the operational approaches depicted in Figure III-1.

b. **Military Strategic Objectives.** The military strategic objectives provide a way to achieve the national strategic aims (end state). The military strategic objectives are:

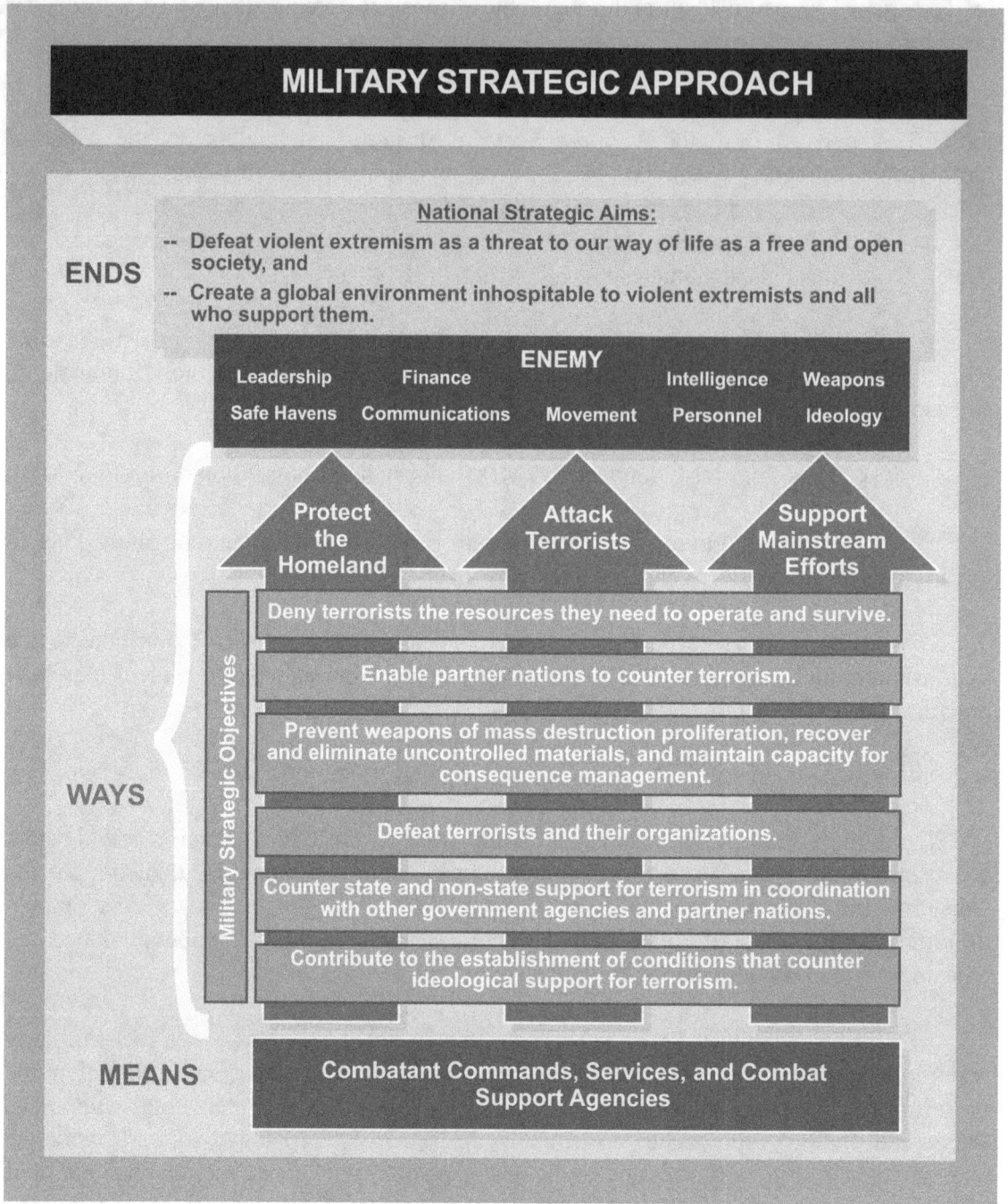

Figure I-2. Military Strategic Approach

(1) **Deny Terrorists the Resources They Need to Operate and Survive.** Understanding the critical nodes and linkages of the terrorists' networks is critical. At the national military level, efforts are focused on identifying global linkages among terrorist networks, and then to arranging regional actions that will create detrimental effects network-wide. Because the terrorists are located in many countries around the world, much of the effort against them will have to be made by those countries with the necessary encouragement and assistance of the United States.

(2) **Enable Partner Nations to Counter Terrorism.** Terrorist groups based in a remote, relatively inaccessible country can still pose a major threat to the United States and its interests. Countering terrorism requires a worldwide, continuous, and comprehensive effort to create a global environment inhospitable to violent extremists and all who support them. The United States must also continue to encourage and assist bilateral and multilateral regional partnerships among states that can work together in CbT.

(3) **Prevent WMD Proliferation, Recover and Eliminate Uncontrolled Materials, and Maintain Capacity for Consequence Management (CM).** Important to the terrorist's success is recognition as a credible opponent. The terrorists gain credibility if they are able to obtain and use WMD or successfully employ technology to achieve their goals. Military activities include efforts to detect and monitor WMD acquisition and development (nonproliferation); conduct WMD interdiction or WMD offensive operations against terrorists armed with WMD capabilities (WMD, delivery systems, associated technology, expertise and material) (counterproliferation); conduct security cooperation activities; and coordinate CM operations (e.g., logistics, health service support, and decontamination activities). All of these efforts also serve to protect the homeland.

(4) **Defeat Terrorists and Their Organizations.** This military strategic objective directly addresses the terrorist's ability to continue global terrorist operations. This requires continuous military operations to develop the situation and generate the intelligence that allows the United States to attack global terrorist organizations. This intelligence supports the first objective of military operations against the terrorists: find the terrorist. Once the situation is effectively developed, military operations may be authorized to capture or kill senior leadership and senior operatives, eliminate safe havens, destroy training camps and resources, capture or kill cell members (foot soldiers), and disrupt recruiting and indoctrination efforts. Emphasis is placed on operating with and training PNs to achieve this objective, however the United States must also be prepared to operate unilaterally, if necessary.

(5) **Counter State and Non-State Support for Terrorism in Coordination with Other Government Agencies (OGAs) and PNs.** State sponsorship provides violent extremists access to key resources, including fronts for illegal activities. Non-state supporters may be financial supporters, such as charities and criminal organizations that directly or indirectly support or benefit from terrorist organizations. To counter these threats, US and PN activities include, among others: intelligence operations to identify state sponsors and non-state supporters; operations to eliminate terrorists and their direct supporters; and to interdict their resources (including WMD and their components); CT, counterinsurgency (COIN), counternarcotics efforts, and participation in exercises and capability demonstrations to dissuade and coerce states and non-state entities. In certain circumstances, the military can lead efforts to oust regimes that support terrorists.

(6) **Contribute to the Establishment of Conditions that Counter Ideological Support for Terrorism.** Countering ideological support for terrorism attacks the enemy's strategic COG - extremist ideology. Although DOD is not the lead federal agency for this

effort, the US military can contribute significantly. As examples, the military may be directed to take actions to bolster the security, confidence, and other institutional capabilities of those who oppose violent extremists. Military actions can shake the confidence of violent extremists, expose their false statements and corruption (e.g., through an active public affairs [PA] program), and otherwise diminish their ability to effectively convey their messages of antagonism, violence, and intimidation (e.g., information operations [IO]).

5. Prioritized Strategic End States for the Global War on Terrorism

The strategy and planning guidance is maintained within the functional planning guidance of the GEF while the more specific planning tasks are in the JSCP. Planning starts with the overarching *National Defense Strategy* from which the GEF derives prioritized regional and functional strategic end states. The strategic campaign framework for CT (see Chapter III, "Operational Approaches") and the following current functional end states for the global war on terrorism are contained in the GEF:

a. End State 1. Organizations committed to violent extremism no longer have the capability or intent to strike globally and catastrophically and their capacity to strike is outweighed by the capacity of local governments to counter and defeat them.

b. End State 2. Key states deny the enemy the resources needed to operate and survive. In particular, key states have reduced ungoverned or under governed areas that violent extremists seek to exploit.

c. End State 3. Terrorists, violent extremists, and their supporters are prevented from obtaining, developing, distributing, or using WMD.

d. End State 4. The global environment is inhospitable to terrorism and violent extremism.

(1) Violent extremism is denounced, terrorism activity is criminalized, and sanctions or use of force are supported to thwart or respond to a terrorist attack.

(2) Muslims reject violent extremism and there is popular support for peaceful political and non-extremist political models within the Muslim world.

(3) Based on a shared understanding of terrorist challenges, allies and partners work actively with the United States in pursuing complementary strategies to address them.

(4) States and non-state entities either do not support terrorism or are deterred from supporting terrorism.

6. Irregular Warfare

a. IW is a violent struggle among state and non-state actors for legitimacy and influence over the relevant populations. IW favors indirect approaches and asymmetric means, though it may involve the full range of military and other capabilities, in order to erode an adversary's power, influence, and will.

b. CT is an activity of IW. IW involves a variety of operations and activities that occur in isolation or combined with conventional force operations. An adversary using irregular methods typically will endeavor to wage protracted operations in an attempt to break the will of their opponent and influence relevant populations. Activities applicable to IW include, but are not limited to: foreign internal defense (FID), security force assistance (SFA), COIN, CT, unconventional warfare (UW), stability operations, strategic communication (SC), psychological operations (PSYOP), IO, civil-military operations (CMO), intelligence and counterintelligence, and law enforcement.

c. The focus of IW is on the relevant population and not military platforms or armed forces, as it is in traditional war. IW is a struggle for legitimacy and influence over a population from which its authority to act originates, and is conferred upon either its government or leadership. IW depends not just on military prowess, but also an understanding of such social dynamics as tribal politics, social networks, religious influences, and cultural mores. Therefore, the key to success in IW comes from the ability of a group or organization to influence populations to gain or enhance political authority. Governance is the mechanism through which those political authorities serve the needs of the population. Terrorist and insurgent organizations may seek to attack and disrupt governments and their supporting ideology as a means to erode legitimacy. Hence, all parties seek to undermine their adversaries' legitimacy in order to isolate them physically and psychologically from the relevant populations. At the same time, terrorist and insurgents also seek to bolster their own legitimacy and credibility with those same populations. However, defeating terrorist organizations usually requires maintaining the legitimacy and enhancing the credibility of a political authority to support and govern the relevant population. These actions serve as a means to eliminate terrorist safe havens and set favorable conditions in which direct action can more effectively dismantle or neutralize the terrorist organizations.

d. Successful CT requires stable, long-term engagement to develop comprehensive knowledge of the global and regional environments and provide security and stability for key populations. However, security and stability cannot be provided by military operations alone. As a major IW activity, CT efforts should include all instruments of national power to undermine an adversary's power and will, and its credibility and legitimacy to influence the relevant population. Terrorists use physical or psychological violence to disrupt the capabilities of political authorities to govern. Terrorists seek safe haven within un-governed or under-governed areas. These areas can be decisive points in the CT effort — especially if the terrorist organization migrates towards insurgency tactics and seeks to fulfill governance functions as a means of gaining legitimacy from the population. Security, then, becomes a critical element of any plan to defeat a terrorist network; because without it, a terrorist can gain significant influence by inducing and/or exploiting a population's grievances.

e. IW activities such as CT often will be led by a USG agency other than the DOD. The complex nature of terrorist organizations and their focus on population coercion require joint force commanders (JFCs) to synchronize operations with the activities of the interagency and PN teams to achieve a unity of effort beyond that traditionally associated with direct action CT missions. CT operations require JFCs and their staffs to work closely with interagency and multinational counterparts during all stages of planning and execution to achieve unified action and ensure that actions taken by one organization complement the actions of others.

f. For long-term CT campaigns/operations, an indirect approach for continual shaping and stabilizing should be synchronized with direct approach actions. All US efforts should be integrated with those of the PN in a global and regional context. These efforts require patience, coupled with consistent and persistent messages describing the USG focus on and support of the relevant populations and their legitimate government. **Paramount to success in planning CT is an appreciation for the basic human physiological, safety, and security needs as motivating factors common to all populations**. The extent to which the USG and other regional and global partners can provide the basis for the relevant population to meet these human needs will affect the degree of popular support of and/or noninterference with joint force CT operations.

HUMAN NEEDS PLANNING CONSIDERATIONS FOR COUNTERTERRORISM

People desire a strong degree of security.

People want control over their social and political order, according to the norms and expectations of their culture.

People want meaningful economic activity that enables them to provide a living for their families.

People want a society that reinforces their cultural preferences and allows them to feel pride and a sense of belonging to their group.

Various Sources

---

7. **Doctrinal Foundation for Counterterrorism**

Joint doctrine is inexorably linked to the development of national military strategy. Accordingly, the development of this publication is tied to the *National Strategy for Combating Terrorism*. Additionally, the scope of CT has broadened from the more narrowly defined "offensive measures" typically conducted by SOF to one that incorporates both SOF and conventional forces in a wide range of actions through "direct and indirect approaches" in unified action against violent extremism. Within these approaches, certain joint doctrine already exists. Joint Publication (JP) 1, *Doctrine for the Armed Forces of the United States,* addresses terrorism within the strategic security environment, terrorism as related to IW, and the US military effort in the context of the long war, among other aspects. JP 3-0, *Joint Operations,* discusses the security environment, strategic guidance, and conduct of joint operations of which CT is a part. Other JPs have related discussions, that when refocused on a CT application, provide methodology that facilitates both direct and indirect approaches to countering terrorism. Examples, while not all inclusive, include the following:

a. **JP 3-22, *Foreign Internal Defense (FID).*** Specific CT efforts can be conducted as part of the FID program for a host nation (HN). FID has long been recognized as a means of supporting the CT and COIN efforts of a number of HNs. The same is true when conducting SFA in support of foreign security forces (FSF).

b. **JP 3-07.2, *Antiterrorism.*** Provides the joint doctrine for planning, executing, and assessing joint antiterrorism operations. It also established the CbT framework of which antiterrorism and CT are a part..

c. **JP 3-07.4, *Joint Counterdrug Operations.*** Narcoterrorism is a form of terrorism linked to illicit drug trafficking. Whether terrorism is used to support drug trafficking or funding from drug trafficking is used to support terrorist activities, there is frequently a correlation between joint counterdrug and CT operations.

d. **JP 3-08, *Interorganizational Coordination During Joint Operations.*** The long war cannot be won without effective integration of the CT efforts of OGAs, intergovernmental organizations (IGOs), and nongovernmental organizations (NGOs) as part of unified action with joint forces. JP 3-08 outlines the methodology to accomplish such coordination.

e. **JP 3-13, *Information Operations.*** IO, with its core and supporting activities, provides the flexibility of action through what are now identified as direct and indirect approaches to influence, disrupt, corrupt, or usurp the terrorists' human and automated decision-making processes while protecting our own.

f. **JP 3-13.2, *Psychological Operations.*** PSYOP, as a core IO capability, have proven to be an essential part of the capabilities required for CT, especially in application of the indirect approach to shape, stabilize, and influence the environment in which VEOs operate.

g. **JP 3-16, *Multinational Operations.*** Many aspects of integrating multinational efforts are described, whether through coalitions, alliances, or partnerships, that will be required to fight the long war on terrorism.

h. **JP 3-57, *Civil-Military Operations.*** CMO can support both the direct and indirect approaches to CT. CMO, with its range of activities, can build a nation's capacity to combat terrorism by mitigating the actions of VEOs, helping gain the support of moderate elements, and otherwise create a secure and stable environment.

Intentionally Blank

CHAPTER II
TERRORIST THREATS

The Nature of the Terrorist Threat Today

"We have seen their kind before. They are the heirs of all the murderous ideologies of the 20th century. By sacrificing human life to serve their radical visions—by abandoning every value except the will to power—they follow in the path of fascism, and Nazism, and totalitarianism. And they will follow that path all the way, to where it ends: in history's unmarked grave of discarded lies."

President George W. Bush
Address to a Joint Session of Congress and the American People
September 20, 2001

---

1. Overview

America is at war with extremists who advocate and use violence to gain control over others and threaten our way of life. Violent extremists find it useful to mischaracterize the war as a religious or cultural clash (e.g., between Islam and the West). These violent extremists see the United States and other western societies as primary obstacles to achieving their political ends. The greatest strength of our society is its freedom and openness. The extremist networks will continue to exploit the seams in open societies around the globe, and consequently, the United States and PNs remain vulnerable to terrorist violence designed to undermine those relationships and cause some members to abandon the struggle.

---

terrorism — The calculated use of unlawful violence or threat of unlawful violence to inculcate fear; intended to coerce or to intimidate governments or societies in the pursuit of goals that are generally political, religious, or ideological.

Joint Publication 3-07.2, *Antiterrorism*

---

a. **Nature of the War.** In the years preceding the 9/11 attacks, the United States countered terrorism primarily through diplomacy and law enforcement. The President of the United States declared those attacks acts of war by an enemy that threatens to destroy our freedoms and way of life. **Since that time, the DOD's understanding of the nature of the war and the nature of the enemy continues to mature and evolve.**

(1) Our future efforts will often be executed in the urban areas of various nation states. **As a result, the nature of military operations will be limited by issues of national sovereignty and political risk, all significantly influenced by public opinion at home and abroad.**

(2) The employment of military and other instruments of national power against terrorist organizations is complicated by their secretive nature, widely dispersed resources, support by some populations and governments, often decentralized control, and an almost

---

seamless integration into diverse communities worldwide. The easy availability, speed, and simplicity of global communications, financial transfers, and inter-continental movement of people enable the terrorists' global reach and their capacity to rapidly adapt their tactics and techniques to breach security measures and elude capture.

(3) The conditions that extremist networks exploit to operate and survive have developed over the years, and those conditions must be altered through long-term, sustained operations using both direct and indirect approaches. **Success against transnational terrorism will not occur in a single, defining moment but through a sustained effort to compress the scope and capabilities of terrorist organizations/VEOs, isolating them regionally and individually, and then destroying them within state borders.**

(4) Terrorist networks, such as al-Qaeda, may employ irregular, catastrophic, or disruptive methods to challenge US security interests. **Irregular** threats involve the employment of "unconventional" methods and tactics to counter the traditional advantages of stronger opponents. **Catastrophic** threats involve the acquisition, possession, and potential use of WMD or methods and material producing WMD-like effects. **Disruptive** threats may come from terrorist organizations that develop and use breakthrough technologies to negate current US advantages.

b. **Nature of the Enemy.** Terrorist groups, regardless of ideology, origin, location, or organizational structure have some common basic needs to survive and remain credible to their followers: funding, security, an ability to produce and distribute propaganda, a support infrastructure, an ability to recruit, and the means to conduct violent acts against selected targets.

> **transnational threat.** Any activity, individual, or group not tied to a particular country or region that operates across international boundaries and threatens United States national security or interests.

(1) **The principal enemy is a transnational movement, consisting of extremist organizations, networks, and individuals – and their state and non-state supporters – which uses terrorism for ideological ends.** For example, the brand of terrorism used by Islamic terrorist groups has included the use of children and the mentally challenged as unknowing participants in suicide-bombing attacks against both fellow civilians and government personnel alike. Unlike traditional military adversaries, these **transnational terrorists have shown no tendency to be deterred, adding significantly to the complexity of countering them. This enemy is often educated, absolutely dedicated, highly motivated, and shows little restraint.** Terrorists find freedom of action within physical and virtual safe havens by exploiting modern technology, the population, the civil liberties of the societies they attack, and their extreme ideology. **A common extremist ideology is what links some often disparate organizations into terrorist networks.** Although they may have differing local goals or objectives, **ideological extremism is the foundation of this movement's overall success.** It is the key to motivation, recruitment, and direct and indirect support, **and serves as the basis for justifying terrorist actions no matter how abhorrent.**

(2) **Our secondary enemy is the other collective VEOs that interfere with our CT efforts** and which may transition to overt sponsorship of or active participation in direct action against the United States, our PNs, and our interests.

(3) **Opportunists, Extremists, and Terrorists.** There are a variety of state and non-state actors identified with terrorism that have been generally categorized as opportunists, extremists, and terrorists. **Often, the three may be indistinguishable.**

(a) **Opportunists** are members of criminal organizations (e.g., narco-terrorists), weapon proliferators, or state sponsors, who undercut the rule of law and governmental legitimacy, contributing to an environment of corruption and violence. Opportunists take advantage of opportunities as they arise. They often allow the existence of terrorist safe havens and sanctuaries in various regions of the world or provide mutual support to satisfy other interests. The United States is just beginning to understand the collusive nature of this criminal-extremist nexus—a convergence of opportunists' and extremists' interests. **A key danger of the association are terrorists/extremists seeking to obtain and use, or threaten to use, WMD,** may find their efforts assisted by those opportunists who might not endorse the extremists' views or methods but who are merely seeking financial gain.

> *"In addition to known state proliferators, there is a dangerous new breed of non-state sponsored actors who provide technology and materials for profit such as Pakistani nuclear scientist A.Q. Khan, who developed a matured transnational nuclear proliferation network selling sensitive technology and weapons of mass destruction (WMD)-related materials to any rogue nation or organization willing to pay."*
>
> **US Department of State, Office of the Coordinator for Counterterrorism, Country Reports on Terrorism, *The Global Challenge of WMD Terrorism***

(b) **Extremists** are those who seek to force their ideological beliefs on others. They oppose—in principle and practice — the right of people to choose how to live and how to organize their societies; and support the murder of ordinary people to advance their extremist ideological objectives. **Many violent extremists, because of the degree to which they carry their violence, are best described as terrorists.** VEO is a characterization of organized extremists who may not be part of a transnational terrorist network, the primary enemy, but are organized and dangerous enough to be the secondary enemy in the long war on terrorism.

(c) The term **terrorist** refers to those who commit acts of terrorism.

c. **Enemy COGs and Critical Vulnerabilities.** The analysis of the critical capabilities inherent in the adversary's COGs should identify their critical requirements, and in turn, the critical vulnerabilities. **Critical vulnerabilities are those aspects or components of the adversary's critical requirements which are deficient or vulnerable to direct or indirect attack that will create decisive or significant effects.** The networked and cellular structure of global extremist threats requires careful and continuous COG analysis, because a COG can change during the course of an operation. The danger is relying on those "critical factors"—capabilities, requirements, and vulnerabilities—that are not accurate for a given CT operation. **COG and critical vulnerability analysis enable the USG to focus efforts more effectively on the enemy.**

(1) COGs exist at the strategic and operational levels, and may differ for each extremist network or organization. **Normally, at the strategic-level, the COG is an extremist ideology.** This ideology motivates anger and resentment and justifies the use of violence to achieve strategic goals and objectives.

(2) Enemy networks rely on **key resources** to be able to operate and survive, and **some of those may be critical capabilities for the COG**. If attacked, these resources may become critical vulnerabilities for further exploitation. Attacked individually or in combination, the loss of key resources serves to disrupt the enemy's ability to operate. Attacked systematically over time, enemy critical vulnerabilities can be exploited and the operational effectiveness of the network neutralized or degraded. Some of the key resources to all terrorist networks include: leadership, safe havens, funds, communications, weapons, foot soldiers, and ideological support. Additionally, the processes/functions of movement, intelligence, targeting (especially access to targets), and media relations are essential to a terrorist's purpose. JP 2-01.3, *Joint Intelligence Preparation of the Operational Environment*, provides fundamental principles, guidance, and examples on how to determine enemy COGs and critical vulnerabilities.

2. **Terrorist Behaviors, Motivations, and Characteristics**

The following discussion provides an insight into terrorist behaviors at both the individual and group levels, examines the impact of group goals and motivations on terrorist planning and operations, and provides observations of general terrorist characteristics.

a. **Terrorist Behavior.** Terrorism is a rationally selected tactic usually employed in the pursuit of ideological aims. However, some individuals or small violent organizations that employ terrorist means may not always be concerned with particular causes or an avowed ideology. These terrorists may be motivated purely by a desire to commit violent acts. From a psychological behavioral perspective, terrorism may fulfill a compelling need and this form of terrorism treats avowed ideology and political causes as after the fact justification. Another behavioral perspective is one based on rational choice. **Terrorism is a tactic selected after rational consideration of the costs and benefits in order to achieve an objective.**

(1) **Individual Terrorist Behaviors**

(a) **Utopian View.** Some terrorists have utopian goals regardless of their aims. This utopianism expresses itself forcefully as an extreme degree of impatience with the "status quo" of the rest of the world that validates the terrorists' extreme methods. This view commonly perceives a crisis too urgent to be solved other than by the most extreme methods. Alternately, the perception is of a system too corrupt or ineffective to see or adopt the "solution" the terrorist espouses. This sense of desperate impatience with opposition is central to the terrorist worldview. This is true of both the secular and religiously motivated terrorist, although with slightly different perspectives as to how to impose their solutions. There is also a significant impractical element associated with this utopian mindset. Although their goals often involve the transformation of society or a significant reordering of the status quo, individual terrorists, even philosophical or intellectual leaders, are often vague or uncaring as to what the future order of things will look like or how their ideas will be implemented. Change, and the destructive method by which change is brought about, may be much more important than the end result.

(b) **Interaction with Others.** Terrorists interact within their groups at both the member and leadership levels. Individuals forming or joining groups normally adopt the "leader principle" which amounts to unquestioning submission to the group's authority figure. This explains the prevalence of individual leaders with great charisma in many terrorist organizations. Such leaders can demand tremendous sacrifices from subordinates. This type of obedience can cause internal dissension when a leader is at odds with the group or factions arise in the organization. Another adaptation of the individual is accepting an "in-group" (us against the world) mentality. This results in a presumption of automatic morality on the part of the other members of the group, and purity of their cause and goals. Thus, violence is necessary and morally justified and the use of violence becomes a defining characteristic.

(c) **Dehumanization of Nonmembers.** There is a dehumanization of all "out-group" individuals. This dehumanization permits violence to be directed indiscriminately at any target outside the group. Dehumanization also removes some of the stigma regarding the killing of innocents. Another aspect is that by making the oppressed people an abstract concept, it permits the individual terrorist to claim to act on their behalf.

(d) **Lifestyle Attractions.** A terrorist may choose violence as a lifestyle. It can provide emotional, physical, perceived religious, and sometimes social rewards. Emotionally, the intense sense of belonging generated by membership in an illegal group can be satisfying. Physical rewards can include such things as money, authority, and adventure. This lure often can subvert other motives. Social rewards may be a perceived increase in social status or power.

(2) **Behaviors Within Groups.** Terrorists within groups usually have different behaviors collectively than individually. Groups are collectively more daring and ruthless than the individual members. The individual terrorist does not want to appear less committed than the others, and will not object to proposals within the group that they would not consider as an individual. Peer pressure is the norm. Group commitment stresses secrecy and loyalty to the group and ideological intensity abounds. However, this same peer pressure and intensity can sometimes result in the forming of splinter groups or dissenting individual members, and run the risk of compromising the original group's purpose. New causes may evolve as a result. Organizations that experience behavioral

difficulties may tend to increase their level of violence as frustration and low morale develop because of a lack of perceived progress or successful CT operations.

b. **Impact of Terrorist Goals and Motivations on Planning.** Strategies against terrorists require understanding their point of view. Understanding and knowledge of VEO's preferences and capabilities provides a baseline to conduct successful CT operations and promotes the use of active approaches, both direct and indirect, to counter the threat.

(1) **Terrorist Asset Cost Versus Target Value.** Terrorist groups require recruitment, preparation, and integration into the operational structure of the group. Recruits also require extensive vetting to ensure that they are not infiltrators. A group's leadership will not employ assets without weighing the value of the asset, the probability of success, and the potential benefits to the group. For example, suicide bombings are on the increase. This type of terrorist attack provides effective target results for relatively low cost. Normally in a terrorist operation, extensive preoperational surveillance and reconnaissance, exhaustive planning, and sufficient resources will be committed to the operation. The potential risk of exposure of these resources, and the demands on their time, are factored into the equation when deciding to commit to an attack.

(2) **Operational Intent of Terrorism.** At the fundamental level, terrorism is a psychological act that communicates through the medium of violence or the threat of violence. Terrorist strategies are aimed at publicly causing damage to symbols or inspiring fear. Timing, location, and method of attacks accommodate media dissemination and ensure wide-spread reporting to maximize impact. In its purest form, a terrorist operation often will have the goal of manipulating popular perceptions, and strives to achieve this by controlling or dictating media coverage. This control need not be overt, as terrorists analyze and exploit the dynamics of major media outlets and the pressure of the "news cycle." In considering possible terrorist targets, a massive destructive attack launched against a target that does not attract media coverage may not be a suitable target for the intended effect and targeted population. When the attack is meant to influence a population outside of the area of interest to the terrorists (i.e., the US) in order to influence decision making, a small attack against a "media accessible" target may be a more lucrative target than a larger one of less publicity. However, the spread of information technology and its accessibility, the growth of global and regional media outlets, and the sense of a global community make many targets more attractive than they were in the past.

(3) **Ideological and Motivational Influences on Operations.** Ideology and motivation are the primary characteristics that influence the objectives of terrorist operations. Groups with secular ideologies and nonreligious goals often will attempt highly selective and discriminate acts of violence to achieve a specific political aim. This often requires the terrorist group to keep casualties to the minimum amount necessary to attain the objective. This is both to avoid a backlash that might severely damage the organization and to also maintain the appearance of a rational group that has legitimate grievances. By limiting their attacks, the group reduces the risk of undermining external political and economic support. Groups that comprise a "wing" of an insurgency, or are affiliated with sometimes legitimate political organizations often operate under these constraints. The

tensions caused by balancing these considerations are often a prime factor in the development of splinter groups and internal factions within these organizations. In contrast, religiously oriented groups typically attempt to inflict as many casualties as possible. An apocalyptic frame of reference may deem loss of life as irrelevant and encourage mass casualty producing incidents. Losses among this group are of little account because such casualties will reap the benefits of the afterlife. Likewise, nonbelievers, whether they are the intended target or collateral damage, deserve death, because their killing may be considered a moral duty. The type of target selected will often reflect motivations and ideologies. For groups professing secular, political, or social motivations, their targets are highly symbolic of authority. They may also conduct attacks on individuals whom they associate with economic exploitation, social injustice, or political repression. While religious groups also use much of this symbolism, there is a trend to connect it to greater physical devastation. There also is a tendency to add religiously affiliated individuals to the targeting equation. Another common form of symbolism in terrorist targeting is striking on particular anniversaries or commemorative dates.

c. **Terrorist Characteristics.** Singular personality profiles of terrorists do not exist. In general, terrorists often feel alienated from society, have a perceived grievance, or regard themselves as victims of an injustice. The following provides some general characteristics that are fairly common among terrorists.

(1) **Status.** Contrary to a belief that terrorism is a product of poverty and despair, terrorists most commonly originate from middle class backgrounds, with some coming from extreme wealth and privilege. While guerilla fighters and gang members often come from poor and disadvantaged backgrounds, and may adopt terrorism as a tactic, terrorist groups that specifically organize as such generally come from middle and upper social and economic strata. The leadership may use less educated and socially dispossessed people to conduct acts of terrorism. Even within terrorist groups that espouse the virtues of "the people" or "the proletariat," leadership consists of those of middle class backgrounds. This characteristic, however, must be considered within the society from which the terrorist originates.

(2) **Education and Intellect.** In general, terrorists, especially their leaders, are usually of average or better intelligence and have been exposed to advanced education. **Very few terrorists are uneducated or illiterate.** Some leaders of larger terrorist organizations may have minimal education, but that is not the norm. **Terrorist groups increasingly are recruiting members with expertise in areas such as communications, computer programming, engineering, finance, and the sciences.** Among terrorists that have had exposure to higher learning, many are not highly intellectual and are frequently dropouts or possess poor academic records. However, this is subject to the norms of the society from which they originate. Societies where religious fundamentalism is prevalent, the focus of advanced studies may have been in religion or theology.

(3) **Age.** Terrorists tend to be young. Leadership, support, and training cadres can range into the 40- to 50-year-old age groups, but most operational members of terrorist organizations are in the 20- to 35-year-old age group. The amount of practical experience

and training that contributes to making an effective operative is not usually present in individuals younger than the early 20s. Individuals in their teens have been employed as soldiers in guerilla groups, but terrorist organizations tend to not accept extremely young members, although they will use them as nonoperational supporters. **Groups that utilize suicide operations often employ very young individuals as suicide assets, but they likely are not actual members of the organization and are simply coerced or exploited into an operational role.**

(4) **Gender.** The terrorists' gender is predominately male, but not exclusively male, even in groups that are rigorously Islamic. Females in these groups are used to support operations or assist in intelligence gathering. Some fundamentalist Islamic groups, however, may use females in the actual conduct of terrorist operations. In groups where religious constraints do not affect women's roles, female membership may be high and leadership roles within the group are not uncommon. Female suicide bombers have been employed with a growing frequency.

(5) **Appearance.** Terrorists are often unremarkable in individual characteristics and attempts to "profile" likely terrorist groups' members may not be productive. They may not appear out of the ordinary and are capable of normal social behavior and appearance. Over the long term, elements of fanatical behavior or ruthlessness may become evident, but they are typically not immediately obvious to casual observation.

3.   Terrorist Organization

A terrorist organization's structure, membership, resources, and security determine its capabilities, influence, and reach. A general knowledge of the prevalent models of terrorist organizations helps to understand their overall capabilities. **A terrorist organization is characterized by its levels of commitment, the tactical level cellular organization, group organizational structure, and its primary motivation.**

a. **Terrorist Levels of Commitment.** Typically, there are four different levels of commitment within a terrorist organization: **passive supporters, active supporters, cadre, and leadership**. Figure II-1 graphically depicts the ratio of people characterizing each successive level of commitment within terrorist organizations.

(1) **Leaders** provide direction and policy; approve goals and objectives; and provide overarching guidance for operations. Usually leaders rise from within the ranks of any given organization, or create their own organization, and are ruthless, driven, and very operationally oriented in order to accomplish their objectives.

(2) **Cadre** is the nucleus of "active" members, the zealots, who comprise the core of a terrorist organization. This echelon plans and conducts not only operations, but also manages areas of intelligence, finance, logistics, IO, and communications. Mid-level cadres tend to be trainers and technicians such as bomb makers, financiers, and surveillance experts. **Low-level cadres are the bombers and foot soldiers for other types of attacks.**

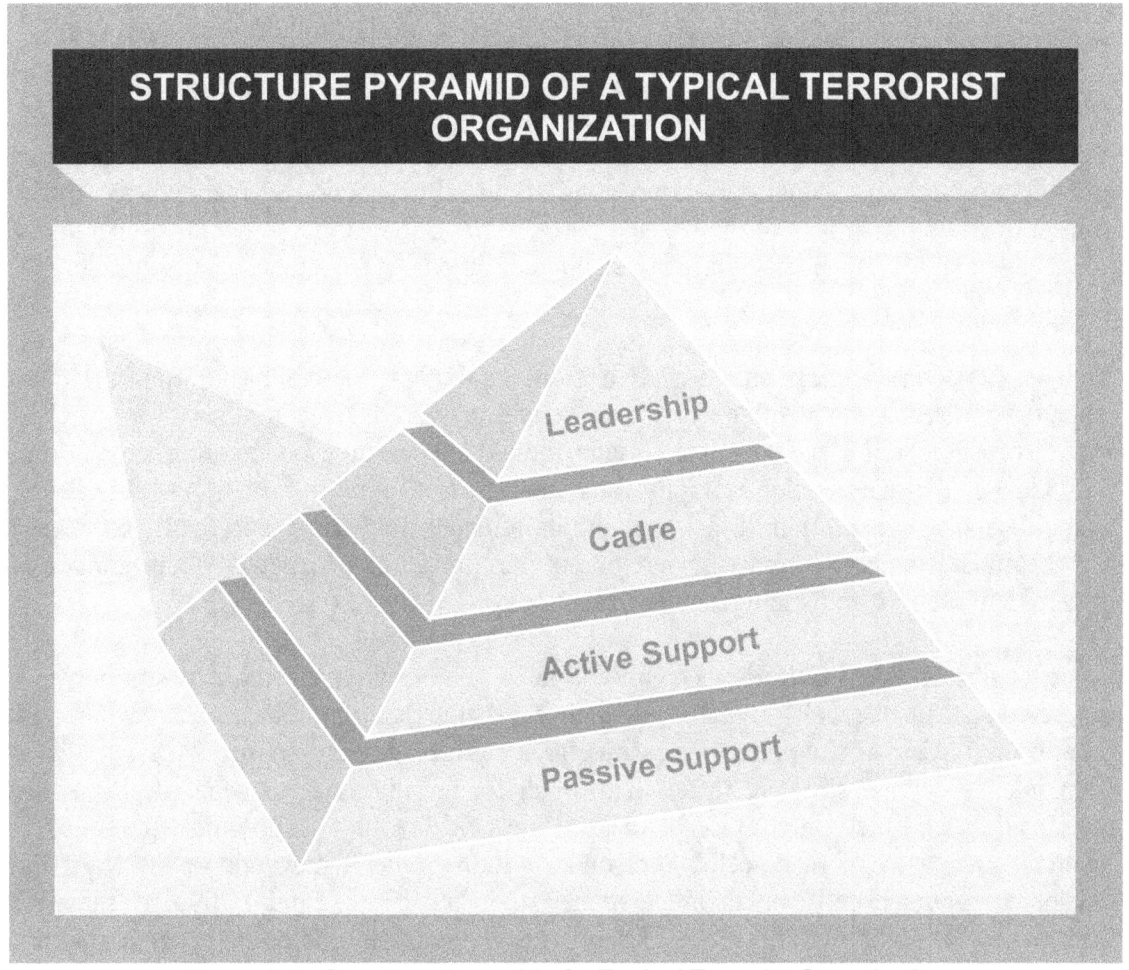

Figure II-1. Structure Pyramid of a Typical Terrorist Organization

(3) **Active supporters** participate in the political, fund-raising, and information activities of the group. Acting as an ally or tacit partner, they may also conduct initial intelligence and surveillance activities, and provide safe houses, financial contributions, medical assistance, and transportation assistance for cadre members. **Usually, they are fully aware of their relationship to the terrorist group but do not commit violent acts.**

(4) **Passive supporters** are typically **individuals or groups that are sympathetic to the announced goals and intentions of the terrorist organization or its ideology,** but are not committed enough to take action. Passive supporters may interact with a front group that hides the overt connection to the terrorist group, or passive supporters may intermingle with active supporters without being aware of what their actual relationship is to the organization. Sometimes fear of reprisal from terrorists compels passive support. Sympathizers can be useful for political activities, fund-raising, and unwitting or coerced assistance in intelligence gathering or other nonviolent activities.

b. Terrorist groups recruit from populations that are sympathetic to their goals or ideology, and often legitimate organizations can serve as recruiting grounds for terrorists.

For example, militant Islamic recruiting has been linked to the schools (Madrassas) established by radical Wahhabi clerics.

(1) Some recruiting may be conducted to acquire personnel with particular skills and qualifications, rather than ideological characteristics. Of particular concern are attempts to recruit personnel with knowledge of WMD production or maintenance and/or current or former members of the US and partner armed forces, both as trained operatives, and as agents-in-place. Recruiting may also occur among groups that feel disenfranchised such as prisoners.

(2) Recruiting can gain operatives from many diverse social backgrounds. Radical behavior or direct actions with terrorism may develop over years or decades. Some groups will also use coercion and leverage to gain limited or one-time cooperation from useful individuals. This cooperation can range anywhere from gaining information to conducting a suicide bombing operation. Blackmail and intimidation (e.g., threats to family members) are the most common forms of coercion. Coercion is often directed at personnel in government security and intelligence organizations.

c. **Tactical-level Cellular Organization.** The smallest elements of terrorist organizations are the cells at the tactical level — the building blocks for the terrorist organization. **One of the primary reasons for a cellular or compartmental structure is security.** A cellular structure makes it difficult for an adversary to penetrate the entire organization, and the compromise or loss of one cell does not compromise the identity, location, or actions of other cells. Personnel within one cell may not be aware of the existence of other cells or their personnel and, therefore, cannot divulge sensitive information to infiltrators or captors. Terrorists may organize cells based on tribal, family, or employment relationships, on a geographic basis, or by specific functions such as direct action or intelligence. Some cells may be multifunctional. The terrorist group uses the cells to control its members. Cell members remain in close contact with each other in order to provide emotional support and to prevent desertion or breach of security procedures. The cell leader is normally the only person who communicates and coordinates with higher levels and other cells. Thus, a local terrorist group could, unwittingly, be part of a larger transnational or international network.

d. **Group Organizational Structure.** There are two typical organizational structures used by terrorist groups: **networked and hierarchical** (see Figure II-2). Newer groups tend to organize or adapt to the network model. Terrorist groups associated with political organizations and activities prefer the more structured and centralized control of the hierarchical structure to coordinate their violent action with political action (e.g., traditional Leninist or Maoist groups) because strict control of activities can be difficult to enforce in a networked organization. Within either of those two larger organizational structures, however, **virtually all terrorist groups use variants of "cellular organizations" (i.e., compartmentalization) at the tactical level to enhance security and to organize for operations.**

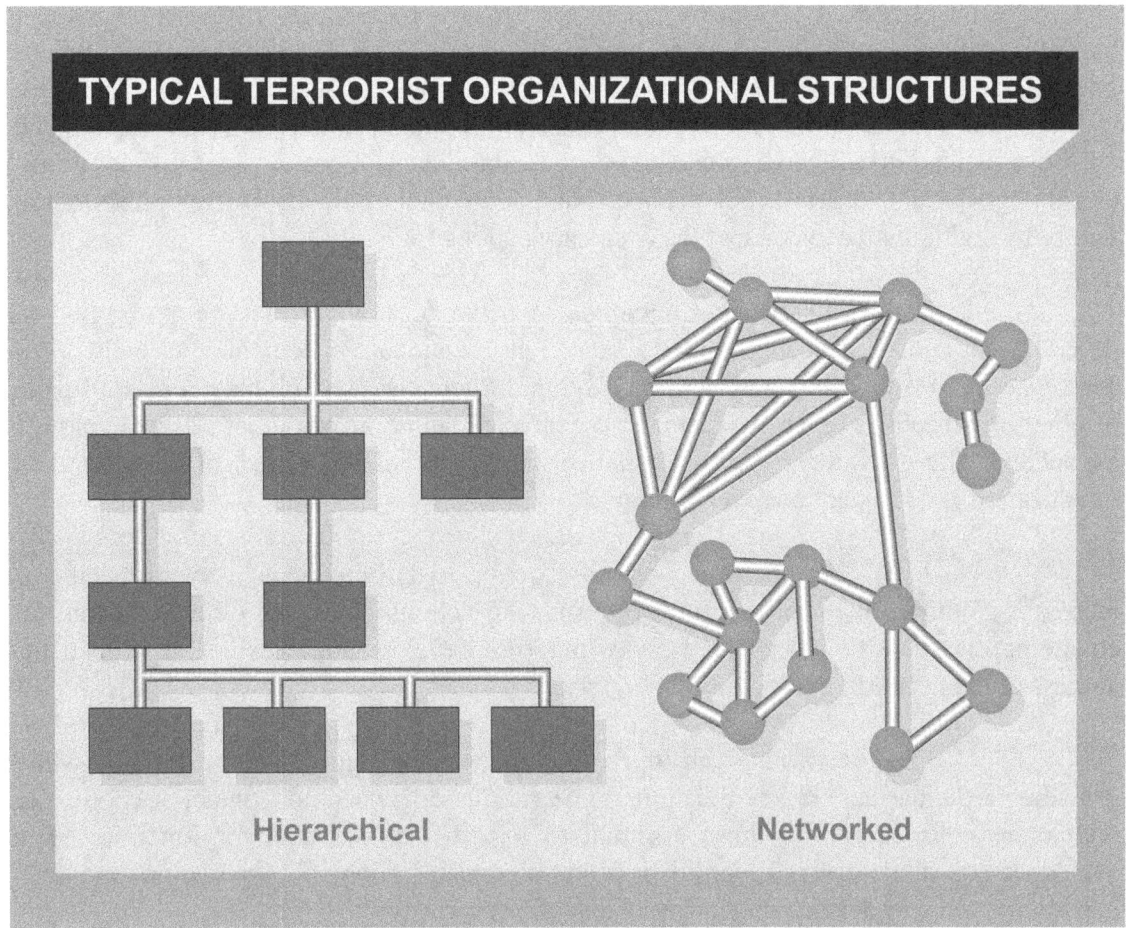

Figure II-2. Typical Terrorist Organizational Structures

(1) **Hierarchical Structure.** These organizations have a well-defined vertical chain of command and responsibility. Information flows up and down organizational channels that correspond to these vertical chains, but may not move horizontally through the organization. This is more traditional, and is common of groups that are well established with a command and support structure. Hierarchical organizations feature greater specialization of functions in their subordinate cells (support, operations, intelligence). Normally, only the cell leader has knowledge of other cells or contacts, and only senior leadership has visibility of the entire organization. In the past, some significant "traditional" terrorist organizations influenced by revolutionary theory or ideology used this structure: Japanese Red Army, the Red Army Faction in Germany, the Red Brigades in Italy, as well as ethno-nationalist terrorist movements such as the Palestine Liberation Organization, and the Provisional Irish Republican Army (IRA). These organizations had a clearly defined set of political, social or economic objectives, and tailored aspects of their organizations (such as a "political" wing or "social welfare" group) to facilitate their success. The necessity to coordinate actions between various "fronts," some political and allegedly nonviolent, and the use of violence by terrorists and some insurgents, favored a strong hierarchical structure.

(2) **Networked Structure.** Terrorists are now increasingly part of a far broader but indistinct system of networks than previously experienced. Groups based on religious or single-issue motives lack a specific political or nationalistic agenda and therefore have less need for a hierarchical structure to coordinate their actions. Instead, they can depend on loose affiliation with like-minded groups or individuals from a variety of locations. General goals and targets are announced, and individuals or cells are expected to use flexibility and initiative to conduct the necessary actions.

(a) **Basic Network Concepts.** A network structure may be a variation of several basic nodal concepts, a node being an individual, a cell, another networked organization, or even a hierarchical organization. A terrorist network may consist of parts of other organizations (even governments), which are acting in ways that can be exploited to achieve the network's organizational goals. The effectiveness of a networked organization is dependent on several things.

<u>1</u>. Network effectiveness requires a unifying idea, concern, goal, or ideology. Without that unifier, networks can take actions or pursue objectives that are counterproductive, and independent nodes may not develop the necessary synergism for success of the network.

<u>2</u>. Networks can distribute the responsibility for operations while providing redundancies for key functions. The various cells need not contact or coordinate with other cells except for those essential to a particular operation or function. The avoidance of unnecessary coordination or command approval for action provides deniability to the leadership and enhances operations security.

<u>3</u>. Networks need not be dependent on the latest information technology to be effective. The organizational structure and the flow of information inside the organization (i.e., their information management plan) are the defining aspects of networks. While information technology can make networks more effective, low-technology means such as couriers and landline telephones can enable networks to operate effectively.

<u>4</u>. Changes in terrorist leadership, whether through generational transition or as a response to enhanced security operations, may signal significant adjustments to terrorist group organizational priorities and its means of conducting terrorism.

(b) **Basic Types of Networks.** There are three basic types of network structures, depending on the ways in which elements (nodes) are linked to other elements of the structure: the chain, hub (or star and wheel), and all-channel. A terrorist group may also employ a hybrid structure that combines elements of more than one network type. For example, a transnational terrorist organization might use chain networks for its money-laundering activities, tied to a hub network handling financial matters, tied, in turn, to an all-channel leadership network to direct the use of the funds into the operational activities of a hub network conducting pre-targeting surveillance and reconnaissance. Organizational structure that may appear very complex during initial assessments of terrorist groups may be more understandable when viewed in the context of chain, hub variants, or all channel networks.

1. **Chain.** Each node links to the node next in sequence and communication between the nodes is by passing information along the line. This organization is typical among networks that have a common function such as smuggling goods and people or laundering money.

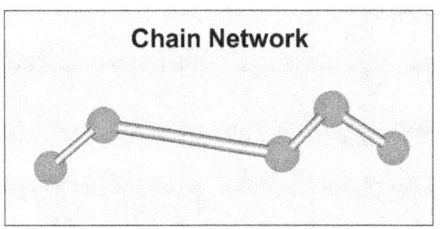

2. **Hub or Star and Wheel.** Outer nodes communicate with one central node, which may not be the leader or decision maker for the network. A variation of the hub is a wheel design where the outer nodes communicate with one or two other outer nodes in addition to the hub. A wheel configuration is common for a financial or economic network.

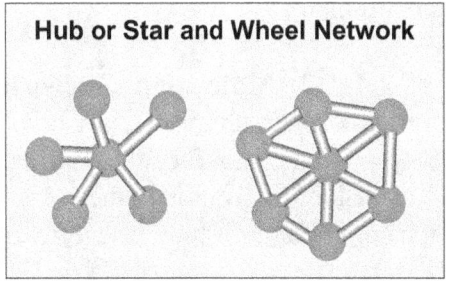

3. **All-Channel.** All nodes are connected to each other. The network is organizationally "flat," meaning there is no hierarchical command structure above it. Command and control is distributed within the network. This is communication intensive and can be a security problem if the linkages can be identified or reconstructed. However, the lack of an identifiable "head" confounds the targeting and disrupting efforts normally effective against hierarchies.

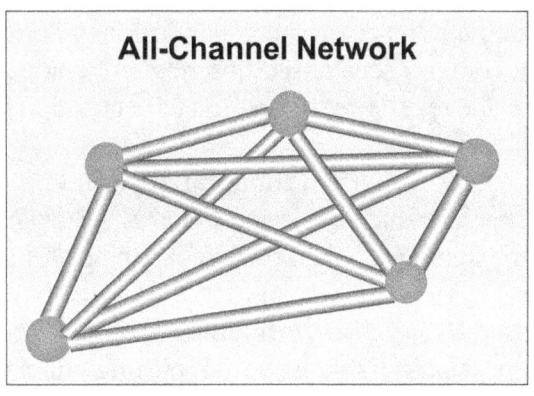

e. **Categories of Terrorist Organizations.** There are many different categories of terrorism and terrorist groups. **These categories serve to differentiate terrorist organizations according to specific criteria, which are usually related to the field or specialty of whoever is selecting the categories.** Also, some categories are simply labels appended arbitrarily, often by the media. For example, every terrorist organization is by definition "radical," as terrorist tactics are not the norm for the mainstream of any group. Much of current terrorism can be described as being based on a universal political ideology or religious dogma, which is in contrast to traditional nationalist-ethnic terrorism that was more prominent in the past.

(1) **Government Affiliation Categories.** Categorizing terrorist groups by their affiliation with governments provides indications of their means for intelligence, operations, and access to types of weapons. **Joint doctrine identifies three affiliations: non-state supported, state-supported, and state-directed terrorist groups.**

(a) **Non-state supported.** These are terrorist groups that operate autonomously, receiving no significant support from any government.

(b) **State-supported.** These are groups that generally operate independently but receive support from one or more governments. Sometimes the support is passive or submissive as the government allows the terrorist group a safe haven within the country.

(c) **State-directed.** These groups operate as an agent of a government and receive substantial intelligence, logistic, and operational support from the sponsoring government.

(2) **Motivation Categories.** Motivation categories describe terrorist groups in terms of their ultimate goals or objectives. While political or religious ideologies will determine the "how" of the conflict, and the sort of society that will arise from a successful conclusion, motivation is the "what" in terms of end state or measure of success. Some of the common motivation categories are:

(a) **Separatist.** Separatist groups desire separation from existing entities through independence, political autonomy, or religious freedom or domination. The ideologies separatists subscribe to include social justice or equity, anti-imperialism, as well as the resistance to conquest or occupation by a foreign power.

(b) **Ethnocentric.** Groups of this persuasion view race as the defining characteristic of a society and a select group is often perceived superior because of its inherent racial characteristics. Ethnicity, therefore, becomes a basis of cohesion.

(c) **Nationalistic.** The loyalty and devotion to a nation, and the national consciousness derived from placing one nation's culture and interests above those of other nations or groups is the motivating factor behind these groups. This can find expression in the creation of a new nation, or in splitting away part of an existing state to join with another that shares the perceived "national" identity.

(d) **Revolutionary.** These groups are dedicated to the overthrow of an established order and replacing it with a new political or social structure. Although often associated with communist political ideologies, this is not always the case, and other political movements can advocate revolutionary methods to achieve their goals.

(3) **Ideological Categories.** Ideological categories describe the political, religious, or social orientation of the group. While some groups will be seriously committed to their avowed ideologies, for others, ideology is poorly understood, and primarily a justification for their actions to outsiders or sympathizers. It is a common misperception to believe that ideological considerations will prevent terrorists from accepting assistance or coordinating activities with terrorists or states on the opposite side of the religious or political spectrum. Quite often terrorists with differing ideologies have

more in common with each other than with the mainstream society they oppose. Common ideological categories include:

(a) **Political.** Political ideologies are concerned with the structure and organization of the forms of government and communities. While observers outside terrorist organizations may stress differences in political ideology, the activities of groups that are diametrically opposed on the political spectrum are similar to each other in practice.

<u>1.</u> **Right-wing.** These groups are associated with the reactionary or conservative side of the political spectrum, and often, but not exclusively, are associated with fascism or neo-Nazism. Despite this, right-wing extremists can be every bit as revolutionary in intent as other groups, the difference being that their intent is to replace existing forms of government with a particular brand of authoritarian rule.

<u>2.</u> **Left-wing.** These groups are usually associated with revolutionary socialism or variants of communism (e.g., Maoist, Marxist-Leninist). With the demise of many communist regimes, and the gradual liberalization of the remainder towards capitalism, left-wing rhetoric can often move towards and merge with anarchistic thought.

<u>3.</u> **Anarchist.** Anarchist groups are antiauthority or antigovernment, and strongly support individual liberty and voluntary association of cooperative groups. Often blending anticapitalism and populist or communist-like messages, modern anarchists tend to neglect the issue of what will replace the current form of government. They generally promote small communities as the highest form of political organization necessary or desirable. Currently, anarchism is the ideology of choice for many individuals and small groups that have no particular dedication to any ideology, and are looking for a convenient philosophy to justify their actions.

(b) **Religious.** Religiously inspired terrorism is on the rise, with over a forty percent increase of total international terrorist groups espousing religious motivation since 1980. While Islamic terrorists and organizations have been the most active, and the greatest recent threat to the United States, all of the major world religions have extremists that have taken up violence to further their perceived religious goals. Religiously motivated terrorists seek justification of their objectives from religious authorities to promote their cause as infallible and nonnegotiable.

<u>1.</u> Religious motivations can also be tied to ethnic and nationalist identities, such as Kashmiri separatists who combine their desire to break away from India with the religious conflict between Islam and Hinduism. The conflict in Northern Ireland also provides an example of the mingling of religious identity with nationalist motivations. There are frequently instances where groups with the same general goal, such as Kashmiri independence, will engage in conflict over the nature of that goal (religious or secular government).

<u>2.</u> Numerous religious denominations have either seen activists commit terrorism in their name, or spawned cults professing adherence to the larger religion while

following unique interpretations of that particular religion's dogma. Cults that adopt terrorism are often apocalyptic in their worldview, and are extremely dangerous and unpredictable. Of note, religiously inspired cults executed the first confirmed uses of biological and chemical nerve agents by terrorists.

(c) **Social.** Often particular social policies or issues will be so contentious that they will incite extremist behavior and terrorism. Frequently this is referred to as "single issue" or "special interest" terrorism.

(d) **Location or Geographic Categories.** Geographic designations have been used in the past, and although they are often confusing, and even irrelevant when referring to international and transnational terrorism, they still appear. Often, a geographical association to the area with which the group is primarily concerned will be made. "Mid-Eastern" is an example of this category and came into use as a popular shorthand label for Palestinian and Arab groups in the 1970s and early 1980s. Frequently, these designations are only relevant to the government or state that uses them. However, when tied to particular regions or states, the concepts of domestic and international terrorism can be useful.

<u>1</u>. **Domestic or Indigenous.** These terrorists are "home-grown" and operate within and against their home country. They are frequently tied to extreme social or political factions within a particular society, and focus their efforts specifically on their nation's sociopolitical arena.

<u>2</u>. **International.** Often describing the support and operational reach of a group, "international" and "transnational" are often loosely defined. International groups typically operate in multiple countries, but retain a geographic focus for their activities. For example, Hezbollah has cells worldwide, and has conducted operations in multiple countries, but is primarily focused on influencing the outcome of events in Lebanon and Israel. NOTE: An insurgency-linked terrorist group that routinely crosses an international border to conduct attacks, and then flees to safe haven in a neighboring country, is "international" in the strict sense of the word, but does not compare to groups that habitually operate across regions and continents.

<u>3</u>. **Transnational.** Transnational groups operate internationally, but are not tied to a particular country, or even region. Al-Qaeda is transnational; being made up of many nationalities, having been based out of multiple countries simultaneously, and conducting operations throughout the world. Their objectives affect dozens of countries with differing political systems, religions, ethnic compositions, and national interests.

(4) **Proliferation of Knowledge Between Organizations.** Terrorist groups increase their capabilities through the exchange of knowledge. Military professionals must evaluate potential terrorist threats according to what capabilities they may acquire through known or suspected associations with other groups, or those capabilities that can be acquired through the study and employment of techniques and approaches that have proven

successful for other terrorist organizations. These exchanges occur both directly and indirectly.

(a) Direct exchange occurs when one group provides the other with training or experienced personnel not readily available otherwise. An example of direct exchange is the provision of sophisticated bomb construction expertise by the IRA to less experienced groups. In 2001, three members associated with the IRA were arrested in Colombia for "inter-group terrorist support." Terrorist techniques not previously observed in FARC [Revolutionary Armed Forces of Colombia] operations, such as use of secondary explosive devices, indicated a transfer of IRA tactics and techniques.

(b) To disseminate much of this knowledge, terrorist organizations often develop extensive training initiatives. Al-Qaeda, for instance, has assembled in excess of 10,000 pages of written training material, more than 100 hours of training videos, a global network of training camps, and considerable amounts of training material that can be distributed either via hard copy or the Internet.

(c) Indirect transfer of knowledge occurs when one group carries out a successful operation and is studied and emulated by others. The explosion of hijacking operations in the 1970s, and the similar proliferation of hostage taking in the 1980s were the result of terrorist groups observing and emulating successful techniques. The widespread use of improvised explosive devices (IEDs), vehicle-borne IEDs, and suicide bombers are further examples of emulated successes.

(d) A development related to this is the proliferation of specialized knowledge useful to terrorists over the last decade. The reductions in military and intelligence establishments after the Cold War have made expertise in sabotage, espionage, small unit tactics, and other useful skills readily available. Similar reductions in research and development institutions make technical and scientific expertise in WMD, information technology, and electronic countermeasures more accessible, either through direct contacts or intermediaries such as rogue or dysfunctional states.

4.   Terrorist Approaches

Terrorist operations typically are planned in great detail with the objectives of minimizing risk, achieving the highest probability of success, and attaining the widest publicity of their actions. Terrorists seek to avoid adversary strengths and concentrate on their weaknesses. Terrorist tactics are aligned with their overall plans which attempt to use the successful achievement of their operational objectives to realize the accomplishment of their strategic goals. Their approaches to planning and execution follow.

a. **Terrorist Approach to Planning and Execution.** Terrorist operational planning can be analyzed according to requirements common to all operations. The planning and operation cycle shown in Figure II-3 is valid for traditional hierarchically organized groups, as well as decentralized "network" type organizations. The differences between the two

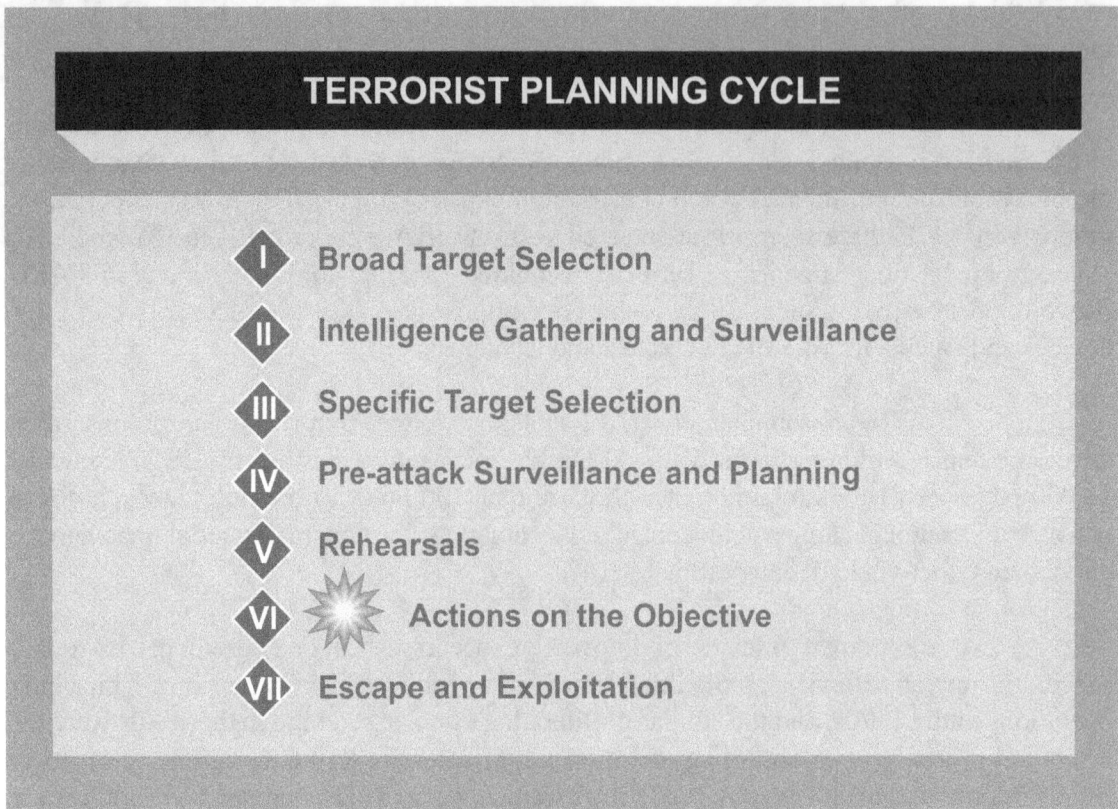

Figure II-3. Terrorist Planning Cycle

organizations are the location of the decision maker at the various steps of the cycle, and the method of task organizing and providing support for the operations.

(1) **Broad Target Selection.** This phase of planning is the collection of information on a large number of potential targets, some of which may never be attacked, or seriously considered for attack. Personnel who are not members of a terrorist organization's cadre, but lower-level active or even passive supporters may be used for data collection and target surveillance.

(a) This phase also includes open source and general information collection. Potential targets are identified through the media, Internet research, and elicitation of unwitting sources.

(b) Potential targets are screened based on symbolic value and their potential to generate high profile media attention. Objectives of the terrorist group influence the selection of a person or facility as a worthy target. This includes the risk and likely casualty figures achieved by the attack. The number of preliminary targets that can be screened is limited only by the capabilities of the group to collect information from sympathizers and open sources. Targets that are considered vulnerable and which would further the terrorist organization's goals are selected for the next phase of intelligence collection.

(2) **Intelligence Gathering and Surveillance.** Targets showing potential vulnerabilities are given a higher priority of effort. The type of surveillance employed depends on the priority and type of target. Elements of information typically gathered include:

(a) **Practices, Procedures, and Routines.** For facilities, this includes scheduled deliveries, work shift changes, identification procedures and other observable routines. For individuals, it can include regularly scheduled errands, appointments, and activities.

(b) **Residence and Workplace.** This category applies primarily to the physical layout and individual activities at the two places the target typically spends the most time.

(c) **Transportation and Routes of Travel.** For individuals, this is the mode of transport and common routes to any regular destination. For facilities and conveyances, it addresses ingress and egress points, types of vehicles allowed on the grounds, or availability of transportation into the target site.

(d) **Security Measures.** Intelligence gathering and surveillance of security measures include a myriad of potential collection areas, depending on the complexity of the security around the target. Presence of a guard force; the reaction time of response units; any hardening of structures, barriers, or sensors; personnel, package, and vehicle screening procedures; and the type and frequency of emergency reaction drills are examples of key collection objectives. This is one of the most important areas of information for attack site selection, since the intent is to bypass and avoid security measures, and be able to strike the target during any period.

(3) **Specific Target Selection.** Target selection for actual planning considers several factors prior to a decision to proceed or not proceed. A decision to proceed requires continued intelligence collection against the chosen target. Targets not receiving immediate consideration will still be collected against for future opportunities. Selection factors include:

(a) Does success affect a larger audience than the immediate victim(s)?

(b) Will the target attract high profile media attention?

(c) Does success make the desired statement to the correct target audience(s)?

(d) Is the effect consistent with objectives of the group?

(e) Does the target provide an advantage to the group by providing the group an opportunity to demonstrate its capabilities?

(f) What are costs versus benefits of conducting the operation?

(4) **Pre-attack Surveillance and Planning.** Members of the actual operational cells begin to appear during this phase. Either trained intelligence and surveillance personnel, or members of the cell organized to conduct the operation conduct this phase of planning. Consequently, the level of intelligence expertise and operational competency increases correspondingly. During this phase, information is gathered on the target's patterns over time, usually days to weeks, sometimes longer depending on the complexity of the target. It allows the attack team to confirm the information gathered from previous surveillance and reconnaissance activities, but with greater focus based upon the planning conducted thus far. The type of surveillance employed depends on the target's activities. The information gained is then used to:

(a) Conduct security studies.

(b) Conduct detailed preparatory operations.

(c) Recruit specialized operatives as needed.

(d) Establish a base of operations in the target area (e.g., safe houses, caches).

(e) Design and test escape routes.

(f) Decide on type of weapon or attack.

(5) **Rehearsals.** As with conventional military operations, rehearsals are conducted to improve the odds of success, confirm planning assumptions, and develop contingencies. Terrorists also rehearse to test security reactions to particular attack profiles. Terrorists use both their own operatives and unwitting people to test target reactions.

(a) Typical rehearsals include:

1. Deployment into target area.

2. Actions on the objective.

3. Escape routes.

4. Equipment and weapon performance.

(b) Tests in the target area are conducted to confirm:

1. Target information gathered to date.

2. Target pattern of activities.

<u>3.</u> Physical layout of target or operation area.

<u>4.</u> Security force reactions (state of alert, timing, size of response, equipment, routes).

(6) **Actions on the Objective.** Once terrorists reach the execution phase of the operation, the odds of success favor the terrorist and are clearly against the target. Terrorists attempt to minimize time spent conducting the actual operation to reduce their vulnerability to discovery or countermeasures. With the exception of barricade-style hostage taking operations, terrorists normally plan to complete their actions before immediate security forces can react. Terrorists conducting planned operations possess important tactical advantages. As the attacker, they possess the initiative, giving them the advantage of surprise; choice of time, place, and conditions of attack; employment of diversions and secondary or follow-on attacks; and employment of security and support positions to neutralize target reaction forces and security measures.

(7) **Escape and Exploitation**

(a) Escape plans are usually well rehearsed and executed. Successful escape further enhances the effect of fear and terror from a successful operation. The exception is a suicide operation, where the impact is enhanced by the willingness to die in achieving the attack. Even in suicide attacks, however, there are usually support personnel and "handlers" who must deliver the suicide asset to the target, and subsequently make their escape.

(b) Exploitation is the primary objective of all terrorist operations. Terrorist operations must be exploited properly and publicized to create their intended effect. Media control measures, prepared statements, and a host of other preparations are made to effectively exploit a successful operation. These are timed to take advantage of media cycles for the selected target audiences (TAs). By quickly capturing and exploiting images themselves, the adversary can rapidly leverage events to influence the public via self-produced media (Internet, radio, television, text messaging, podcast, Weblogs (blogs), etc.) and gain an advantage within the information environment.

(c) Unsuccessful operations are disavowed when possible. The perception that a group has failed severely damages the organization's prestige and makes it appear vulnerable, or worse, ineffective. Once a terrorist organization is perceived as ineffective, it becomes more difficult to impact target audiences or recruit members.

(d) In addition to the impact on the target, successful attacks bring perceived favorable attention, notoriety and support (such as money and recruits) to the terrorist group conducting the operation. If the group conducting the operation subscribes to a revolutionary ideology, they will see each success as gradually inspiring more revolutionary fervor in the population they are attempting to influence. Any success encourages the terrorists to conduct further operations, and improves their ability to do so through increased support and experience.

b. **Terrorist Approach to Operations and Tactics.** The ensuing discussion presents the most common types of terrorist operations and tactics. It is not intended to be an exhaustive discussion of the subject since the combination of methods and approaches is virtually unlimited. However, common themes in terrorist operations are surprise, secrecy, innovation, and indirect methods of attack. Terrorist tactics are broad and diverse. Additionally, with the use of the Internet and common training bases, terrorist groups exchange information on tactics that can yield success.

(1) **Terrorist Operational Considerations**

(a) The terrorist utilizes tactics, forces, and weapons specifically tailored to the particular mission. Terrorist operations are unique, in that each is planned for a specific target and effect. Terrorists normally expose only as much of their resources and personnel as are absolutely necessary to accomplish a mission in order to avoid capture or destruction. A conventional military force would approach an operation with plans to concentrate forces and keep excess combat power on hand to meet contingencies, ensure mission success, and prepare for follow-on missions. A terrorist takes a minimal force and relies upon prior planning and reconnaissance to match the force, weapons, and methods to the target. If changes to the target, or unexpected conditions render success unlikely, the terrorist group will most often cancel or postpone the operation, regroup, update its plan, and adapt to whatever conditions are required to ensure a successful operation. For major terrorist operations, mission accomplishment is often followed by a disbanding of the force, a return of terrorists to their cells and covers, and formation of new task groups for future operations.

(b) In addition to adaptive and flexible organizations, terrorists also employ specific equipment built or procured for a particular operation. Because of the lag time between development of a new technology and military acquisition and fielding, terrorists can sometimes procure equipment superior to standardized military models. As an example, instead of purchasing hundreds of identical radios constructed to meet all likely uses, a terrorist group may only procure the quantity it needs of the newest, most capable radio appropriate for the operation. The only real limitation is funding and availability of the equipment when it is needed. As with equipment, terrorist organizations choose weapons that are tailored to the particular operation. If a particular weapon is not available, the terrorist is adept at creating a weapon from available sources to suit the mission.

(c) Although several types of operations may satisfy a particular objective, terrorist groups often develop expertise in one or more types of operations, and less specialization in others.

(2) **Forms of Terrorist Tactics.** Terrorist tactics take many forms. Some are accomplished as independent actions. Others may be undertaken as part of other coordinated activities. The more common types of terrorist tactics are described below and are shown in Figure II-4.

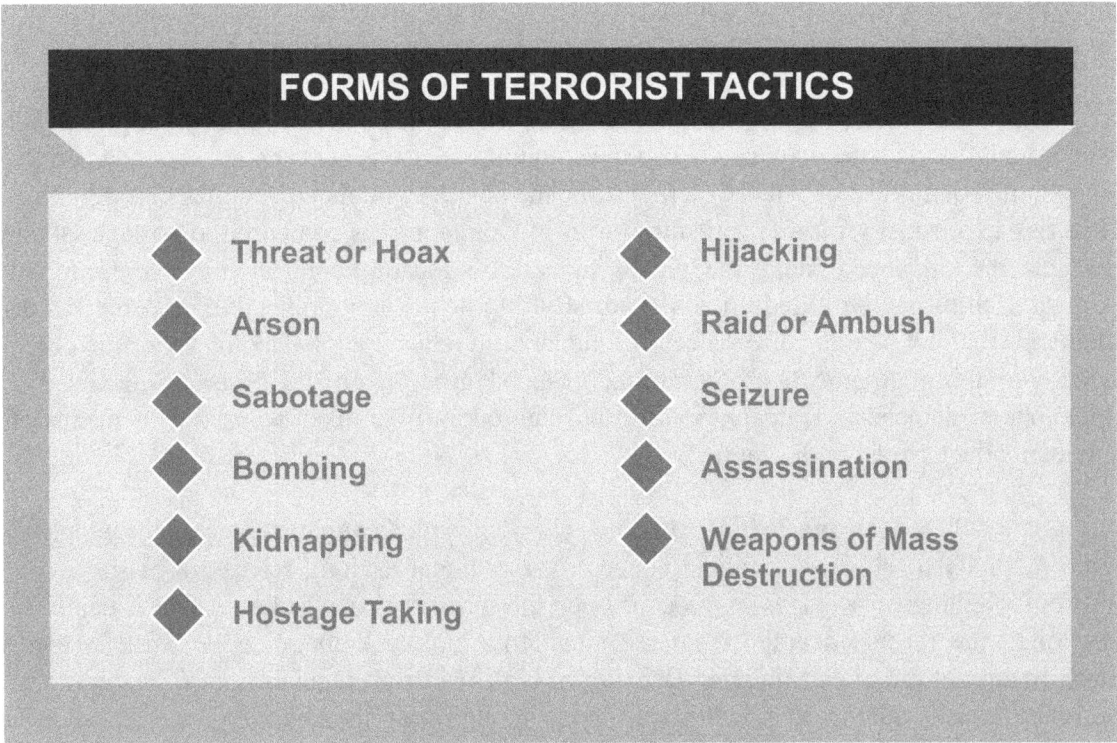

Figure II-4. Forms of Terrorist Tactics

(a) **Threat or Hoax.** Terrorist groups use threats and hoaxes to coerce or preclude actions by a targeted individual or population. Threats and hoaxes can dull the effectiveness of counter or preventive measures when a targeted individual or population loses situational awareness, or disperses finite assets against many possible threats. This tactic also can be used to gain information concerning the target's response to a potential attack. It also can be combined with an actual attack to circumvent fixed security measures as a diversion tactic. While there is limited evidence that terrorists use hoaxes to achieve their aims, the potential exists for them to use them, so JFCs should consider this possibility when conducting CT operations.

(b) **Arson.** Arson is a destructive technique usually used in sabotage operations against property. It is most often used for symbolic attacks and to create economic effects.

(c) **Sabotage.** Sabotage is the planned destruction of the target's equipment or infrastructure. Its purpose is to inflict both psychological and physical damage. Sabotage demonstrates how vulnerable the target is to the terrorist group's actions. Sabotage can have significant economic impacts, as well as the additional effects of creating mass casualties.

(d) **Bombing.** Bombs, to include IEDs, vehicle-borne IEDs, and suicide bombers (wearing explosives or in vehicles with IEDs), are the favored weapon of terrorists. They are highly destructive, are flexible enough to be tailored to the mission, do not require the operator to be present, and have a significant psychological impact. They may be used as a technique to conduct other operations, such as sabotage or assassination, or can simply be a tactic to create terror through destruction and casualties.

(e) **Kidnapping.** Kidnapping is usually conducted against a prominent individual(s) for a specific reason. The most common reasons are ransom, some demanded action such as release of a fellow terrorist; or the desire to publicize a demand or an issue. The risk to terrorist groups is generally lower in kidnapping as compared to hostage taking because the kidnapped victim is typically moved to a location controlled by the group. A kidnap victim may be killed once a terrorist group achieves its objective or perceives its demands will not be met. The success of kidnapping relies upon balancing the value of the victim to the government, organization, or social group with the costs of meeting the kidnappers' demands. Kidnapping (and hostage taking) can also be used as a means of financing the terrorist organization.

(f) **Hostage Taking.** Hostage taking is typically an overt seizure of people to gain publicity for a cause, political concessions, political asylum, release of prisoners, or ransom. Killing of hostages may occur once the terrorist group believes that it has fully exploited the media coverage from the situation. Unlike kidnapping victims, hostages usually are not prominent figures. Because of high risk from retaliation or CT operations, terrorists usually attempt to hold hostages in a neutral or friendly area.

(g) **Hijacking.** Hijacking involves the forceful commandeering of a conveyance. Normally associated with aircraft, it may also include ships, trains, vehicles or other forms of conveyance. The type of hijacking depends on the purpose of the terrorists. Purposes range from hostage taking activities, procuring a means of escape, or as a means of destruction.

(h) **Raid or Ambush.** A terrorist raid is similar in concept to a conventional military operation, but usually is conducted with smaller forces against targets marked for destruction, hijacking, or hostage/barricade operations. In some cases, the raid is designed to allow control of the target for the execution of another operation. An ambush is a surprise attack characterized by violent execution and speed of action. Its objective may be to cause mass casualties, assassinate an individual, or disrupt security operations.

(i) **Seizure.** Seizure of a critical element of infrastructure typically is a physical site of notoriety or importance to a target population, or a media or communications node that could gain widespread attention in one way or another (e.g., pirated broadcasts or disruption of service).

(j) **Assassination.** An assassination is a deliberate action to kill specific, usually prominent, individuals such as political leaders, notable citizens, collaborators, or particularly effective government officials, among others. A terrorist group will assassinate people it cannot intimidate, those who have left the group, people who support the "enemy," or people who have some symbolic significance to the enemy or world community. Terrorist groups may refer to these killings as "punishment" or "justice" as a way of legitimizing them. Assassinations are an effective psychological tool of terrorist tactics.

(k) **WMD.** This category acknowledges a broad range of chemical, biological, radiological, and nuclear (CBRN) weapons. A WMD capability would allow for catastrophic results and could be delivered through numerous means.

(3) **Terrorist IO and Public Relations Activities.** The Internet provides terrorists and extremists the means to spread their radical ideology, an ad hoc means of operational connectivity, and a link to the full-media spectrum for public relations. The Internet facilitates their recruiting, training, logistic support, planning, fund-raising, etc. The internet is also a powerful tool to conduct the equivalent of media facilitated IO against the United States and PNs. Although not yet typical, terrorists may employ electronic attacks to disrupt communications, or banking, or to project disinformation and propaganda in support of their cause. From the terrorist perspective, media coverage is an important measure of the success of a terrorist act and a means of countering US and PN IO and SC activities. News reports, streaming videos on websites, blogs, and editorials can amplify (some unwittingly) the psychological effects of a terrorist incident and aid terrorists in publicizing the event globally to a much wider audience, and potentially gain further recognition of their radical ideology.

Intentionally Blank

CHAPTER III
OPERATIONAL APPROACHES

"In all fighting, the direct method may be used for joining battle, but indirect methods will be needed in order to secure victory. In battle, there are not more than two methods of attack - the direct and the indirect; yet these two in combination give rise to an endless series of maneuvers. The direct and the indirect lead on to each other, in turn. It is like moving in a circle - you never come to an end. Who can exhaust the possibilities of their combination?"

Sun Tzu, *The Art of War*

1. **Nature of the Problem**

a. US superiority in conventional warfighting drives many of our adversaries to avoid direct military confrontation with the United States. **IW, and especially the employment of terrorist tactics, has become the "warfare of choice" for some state and non-state adversaries.** They employ a strategy of physical, economic, and psychological subversion and attrition to undermine, erode, and ultimately exhaust the national power, influence, and will of the United States and its strategic partners. They fight us from amongst the people in protracted struggles for popular support and legitimacy, and limit the utility of our conventional military power.

b. Defeating VEOs and their state and non-state supporters in a protracted struggle will require long-term CT operations concurrently in scores of countries, many of which are not at war with the United States; using all our instruments of national power, and the cooperation and support of foreign security partners.

c. **A low-visibility USG presence in countries where US forces have not traditionally operated**, but where they are needed to train, equip, advise, and support the indigenous security forces (i.e., build PN capacity), supports our national CT strategy and the defeat of designated VEOs. Current efforts being conducted on five continents demonstrates the importance of PNs, having indigenous and surrogate security force capabilities, and operating clandestinely or in a low-visibility manner, to bring security and social, economic, and political stability to unstable areas to influence the global environment. **Security is the foundation for economic and social development and underpins improvements in governance and the rule of law.** These are key pillars for stable, peaceful and prosperous environments that will be less hospitable to terrorists and their sponsors. A strategic goal is to render terrorist organizations incapable of threatening US and PN vital interests and to reduce their threat to a level that can be controlled by local law enforcement actions.

d. **DOD should perform CT operations in unified action.** However, this may not always be possible in some remote, unstable, or hostile environments. **The joint force problem** is twofold: being able **to operate both as a supporting element** to another USG agency lead; **and the supported element** performing military CT operations, as well as CMO in environments where indigenous agencies, IGOs, or OGAs are unable to do so.

2. Strategic Campaign Framework

The strategic campaign framework for CT is composed of three elements: friendly, enemy, and the global environment. **The structure of the campaign uses five logical lines of operations (LOOs) further divided into two categories consisting of efforts applied directly against the enemy and actions applied indirectly to influence the global environment.** These are referred to as direct and indirect approaches. The aims of the strategic campaign are to create a stabilized global environment which is inhospitable to terrorists and their organizations, and to isolate, defeat, and prevent the reemergence of a terrorist threat. The strategic campaign framework is depicted in Figure III-1.

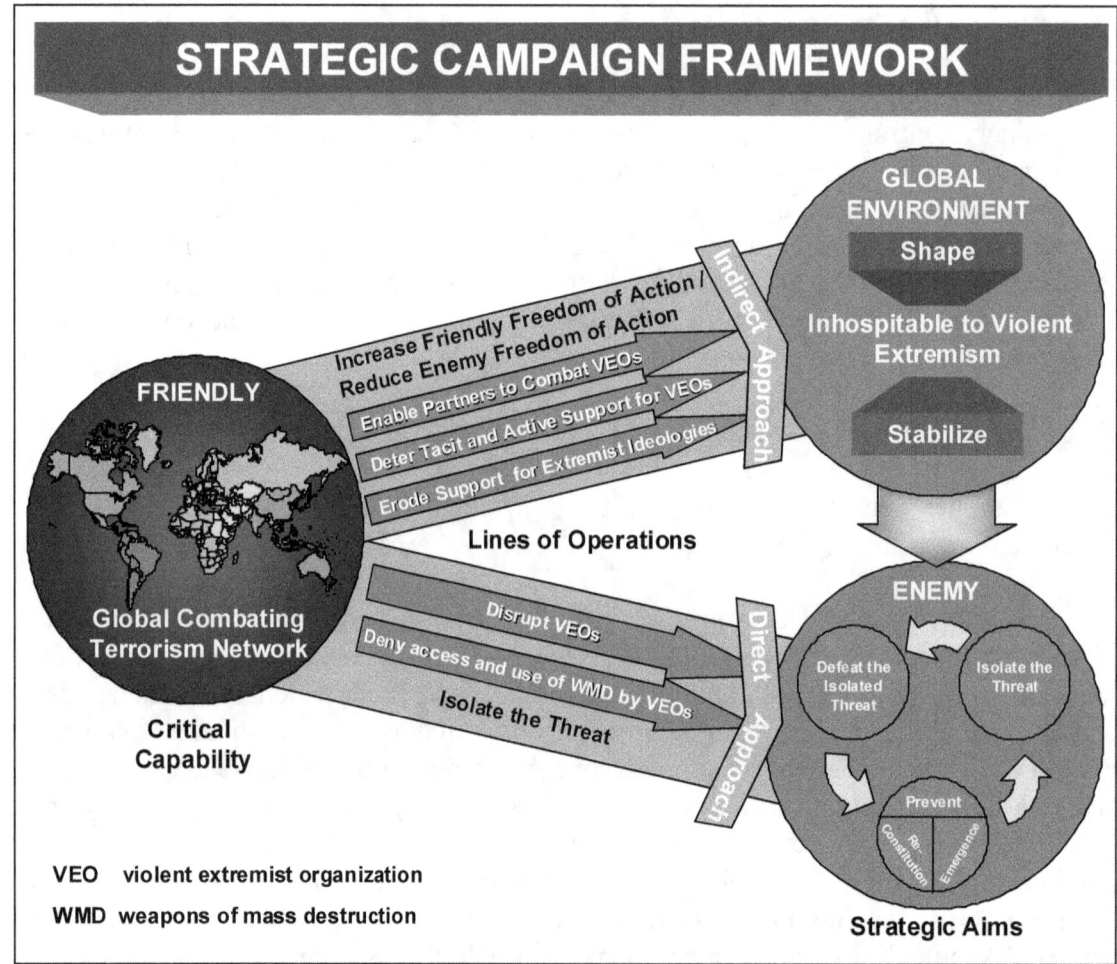

Figure III-1. Strategic Campaign Framework

a. **Strategic Aims.** The strategic aims help define the intermediate conditions to measure progress on a global basis, linking the military strategic objectives with the termination objectives and the end states. These aims include:

(1) Discredit the ideas and beliefs of terrorist organizations and isolate them psychologically from populations.

(2) Build and leverage the capabilities and capacity of USG civilian agencies and foreign security partners to protect populations; gain and/or maintain legitimacy and influence over those populations; and physically isolate terrorist organizations from populations.

(3) Prevent threatened friendly countries from failing by helping them establish and/or maintain effective governance in their ungoverned or under-governed areas.

(4) Encourage and support friendly armed groups opposing or resisting the hostile regimes of countries that support or sponsor terrorism.

(5) Disrupt and defeat terrorist organizations.

(6) Prevent the reconstitution of disrupted or defeated terrorist organizations.

(7) Prevent new terrorist threats from emerging.

b. **Lines of Operations.** Achieving these strategic aims requires integration of the five LOOs within the direct and indirect approaches. The direct approach focuses on actions taken to isolate terrorist organizations in order to disrupt or defeat their operations, reduce their capability to threaten US national security, and prevent their reemergence. The indirect approach focuses on shaping and stabilizing the global environment as a means to erode the support for terrorist organizations and deny them access to the resources they need to survive. The LOOs applied to the indirect approach take more time to have an effect, but will be the decisive actions in the long term. The direct LOOs are: disrupt VEOs; deny access to and the use of WMD by VEOs; the indirect LOOs are: enable partners to combat VEOs; deter tacit and active support for VEOs; and erode support for extremist ideologies.

c. **Global Combating Terrorism Network (GCTN).** Success in CT campaigns is fundamentally driven by the creation of a global environment that is inhospitable to terrorists and their organizations. This end state will be achieved through a coordinated effort integrating US and foreign militaries and agencies, NGOs, and IGOs working together to create a critical mass of capabilities that enable both the direct and indirect approaches necessary to isolate, defeat and prevent the reemergence of terrorist organizations. This coordinated effort creates a critical capability.

d. **A Global Campaign.** The global campaign for CT requires the accomplishment of the strategic aims through joint operations/campaigns by the GCCs in their areas of responsibility (AORs). It allows coordination for strategic unity of effort and purpose, synchronization of the planning, integration of assets, and coordination of the joint operations that may cross AOR boundaries. **Global campaigns mitigate cross-AOR operational risks**. The strategic campaign framework provides for the development of theater and subordinate campaigns and operations and will facilitate integration of many interdependent, cross-AOR missions supporting CT such as security cooperation, intelligence collection, SC, sustainment, and multinational support.

THEATER CAMPAIGN GUIDANCE

Disrupt the timing and tempo of enemy operations

Contain the enemy's actions to their current operational areas

Isolate the enemy from their resources

Neutralize selected capabilities and functions of the enemy

Block the movement of enemy fighters, leaders, and supporters

Interdict the enemy efforts to establish new bases of support and safe havens

**SOURCE: Department of Defense Global
Campaign Plan for the War on Terrorism**

3. **Direct and Indirect Approaches**

a. **Integrated Approaches.** The campaign plan for the war on terrorism makes use of both direct and indirect approaches. These approaches are mutually supporting and integrate the capabilities to concurrently disrupt VEOs operating today and to influence the environment in which they operate to erode their capability and influence in the future. Both approaches are integrated globally from the strategic to tactical levels. **Either or both approaches may be conducted within the scope of a broader campaign as directed by a JFC.** The ability to manage both approaches to harness their synergistic effects is vital to the success of both near- and long-term CT objectives.

SPECIAL OPERATIONS FORCES INTEGRATED APPROACH

In Operation IRAQI FREEDOM, special operations forces (SOF) integrates the direct and indirect approaches on a daily basis. SOF are conducting continual direct action missions to disrupt insurgents and al-Qaida network terrorists, killing or capturing those responsible for committing violence against Iraqis and the multinational force. At the same time, SOF conduct foreign internal defense missions to train and advise the Iraqi Special Operations Forces Brigade and other Iraqi security forces. In fact, the majority of US Army Special Forces (Green Berets) and US Navy SEALs [Sea, Air, and Land forces] in Iraq are partnered with Iraqi units, fighting side-by-side with them, increasingly with Iraqis in the lead, to better enable them to take over all aspects of their country's security in the future. Simultaneously, civil affairs and psychological operations units are engaged in construction, infrastructure rebuilding, and information dissemination operations that positively influence the Iraqi populace and address the underlying conditions of terrorism and the insurgency.

**SOURCE: United States Special Operations
Command Posture Statement 2007**

---

b. **Direct Approach.** The direct approach describes actions taken against terrorists and terrorist organizations. In many situations, the USG will be required to take action against terrorists and their organizations in order to neutralize an imminent threat and degrade the operational capability of a terrorist organization. The goals of the direct approach against terrorists and their organizations are to defeat a specific threat through neutralization/dismantlement of the network (including actors, resources, and support structures) and to prevent the reemergence of a threat once neutralized. However**, the resiliency of terrorist organizations and networks to reconstitute their forces and reorganize their efforts limits the long-term effectiveness of the direct approach as a sole means of countering terrorism**. Specific to the direct approach are operations and activities designed to:

(1) Disrupt terrorists and their organizations. These actions focus on VEO infrastructure and leadership which provide the enemy global access, connectivity, and the resources needed to operate and survive over the long-term.

(2) Deny access to and use of WMD by terrorist organizations. These actions seek to deny acquisition, development, or the use of WMD against the United States or its partners.

(3) An example of a military capability applicable to the direct approach is **direct action**. This action requires a high degree of discrimination and precise use of force to achieve specific objectives. These actions are normally of short duration and conducted in a hostile, denied, or politically sensitive area where a terrorist enclave may exist.

c. **Indirect Approach.** The indirect approach describes the means by which the GCTN can influence the operational environments within which CT campaigns/operations are conducted. This approach usually includes actions taken within LOOs to enable partners to conduct operations against terrorists and their organizations as well as actions taken to shape and stabilize those environments as a means to erode the capabilities of terrorist organizations and degrade their ability to acquire support and sanctuary. The indirect approach combines various operations and activities (e.g., FID, UW, stability operations, CMO, counterintelligence, IO, PSYOP, and SC) that produce synergies designed to:

(1) Enable PNs to combat terrorist organizations. These actions are taken by DOD in support of a larger USG effort to ensure our partners have both the capability and will to effectively conduct long-term operations to defeat terrorist organizations. Our partners have the cultural and historical understanding which when coupled with advanced technology; intelligence, surveillance, and reconnaissance (ISR); and training, can help develop the necessary capability to execute operations within their borders and regionally to defeat terrorism. The realization of this capability for partners to secure their own territory is decisive in a CT campaign.

(2) Deter tacit and active support for terrorism. Actions taken by DOD are part of a larger USG effort to deter state and non-state actors from providing tacit and active

support of terrorist organizations. The goal of the indirect approach is to influence the global environment by shaping and stabilizing it to deny terrorists safe havens and access to population bases that are ripe for terrorist recruiting operations. The indirect approach seeks to change the conditions, ideologies, and motivations which spawn terrorists and to isolate terrorists and their organizations (psychologically and physically) from populations. This will facilitate their subsequent neutralization/dismantlement through the direct approach and prevent their ability to reconstitute. Applications of the indirect approach are long-term efforts that require consistency and persistence in order to have a full effect.

(3) Erode support for terrorist ideologies. Actions within this LOO are part of larger USG efforts to erode legitimacy of terrorist ideologies and neutralize their propaganda and misinformation campaigns which often serve as justification for acts of terrorism. Additionally, these actions seek to reduce support for terrorists over time by alleviating the underlying conditions (e.g., government corruption, poverty, chronic unemployment, and illiteracy), which can be exploited by terrorists.

(4) Examples of military capabilities applicable to the indirect approach are:

(a) **UW.** UW covers a broad range of military and paramilitary operations, normally of long duration conducted through, with, or by indigenous or surrogate forces supported by an external source. Use of these types of forces within the UW umbrella can result in firsthand knowledge and information of terrorist groups and organizations located within the operational area and provide a means for locating and defeating the terrorists in their backyard.

(b) **FID.** Subversion, lawlessness, and insurgency can contribute to the rise of terrorism. While FID is a core task of SOF, CF have established capabilities for FID. FID conducted by CF and SOF can help the HN reduce these contributing factors to terrorism. The FID strategy focuses on building viable political, economic, military, security infrastructure, and social institutions for the needs of the local population. FID operations involve military training and building infrastructure (e.g., schools, roads, and wells) in conjunction with foreign aid programs administered by DOS. Specific CT efforts also can be conducted as part of the FID program for a HN.

1. Bolstering the will of other states to fight terrorism is primarily the responsibility of DOS. Effective FID programs, however, can improve public perceptions of the HN and USG and facilitate more active HN policies to combat terrorism. More directly, military-to-military contacts can help make HN officials advocates of potential operations against terrorist capabilities.

2. In many cases, measures increasing the capacity of a state to fight terrorism also will strengthen its overall internal defense and development program. These measures, not all inclusive, include the following: developing the ability of the HN to break funding streams for criminal and insurgent groups, and prosecute their members; ensuring that HN security personnel have access to appropriate equipment and training to conduct all phases of CT operations; training HN personnel at entry and exit points (including airports,

seaports, and border crossings) to identify and apprehend individuals and materials being used by international/transnational terrorist groups; assist HN security and intelligence agencies in gaining access to international networks that can share information on terrorist activities; and help HNs develop effective judicial systems and minimize corruption and intimidation of officials.

(c) **SFA.** SFA encompasses joint force activities conducted within unified action to train, advise, assist, and equip FSF is support of a partner nation's efforts to generate, employ, and sustain local, HN, or regional security forces and their supporting institutions. This includes activities from ministry level to tactical level units of action, and the national security support base.

(d) **Civil Affairs Operations (CAO).** These operations facilitate CMO which in turn support the overall operation/campaign by enhancing the relationship among military forces, civil authorities, and the private sector in functional specialty areas (i.e., governance, economic stability, infrastructure). Civil affairs (CA) personnel also coordinate with other OGAs, IGOs, NGOs, and the indigenous populations and institutions, all of which are susceptible to terrorist influences. While CAO are conducted during all phases of a campaign, CA can facilitate specific phases by performing in a "first-responder" role by applying these functional specialty skills normally the responsibility of civil government until the HN, in coordination with the USG and its partners, can reestablish the authority of legitimate civil entities.

(e) **PSYOP.** PSYOP actions and activities are planned and conducted to influence foreign audiences in support of USG objectives. This capability is integrated in USG CT efforts to increase the likelihood of success. All PSYOP are governed by explicit authorities that provide for Joint Chiefs of Staff advocacy, interagency coordination and support, and Secretary of Defense (SecDef) approval. During CT operations, PSYOP are used to discredit the terrorist activities and to show the benefits of rejecting terrorism and its associated activities in an effort to gain popular support for the CT operations.

4. Terrorism Threat and Counterterrorism Models

The following models show how extremists can operationally become VEOs and further establish and maintain a network for global terrorism, and how the US-led GCTN uses the strategic LOOs within the direct and indirect approaches to influence/counter the critical enabling components of the terrorism threat.

a. Terrorism Threat Model

(1) To understand the nature of the development of VEOs, the war on terrorism campaign plan uses a circular model (Figure III-2) that represents the four critical enabling components in the cycle of terrorist operations that facilitates development of a global terrorism network.

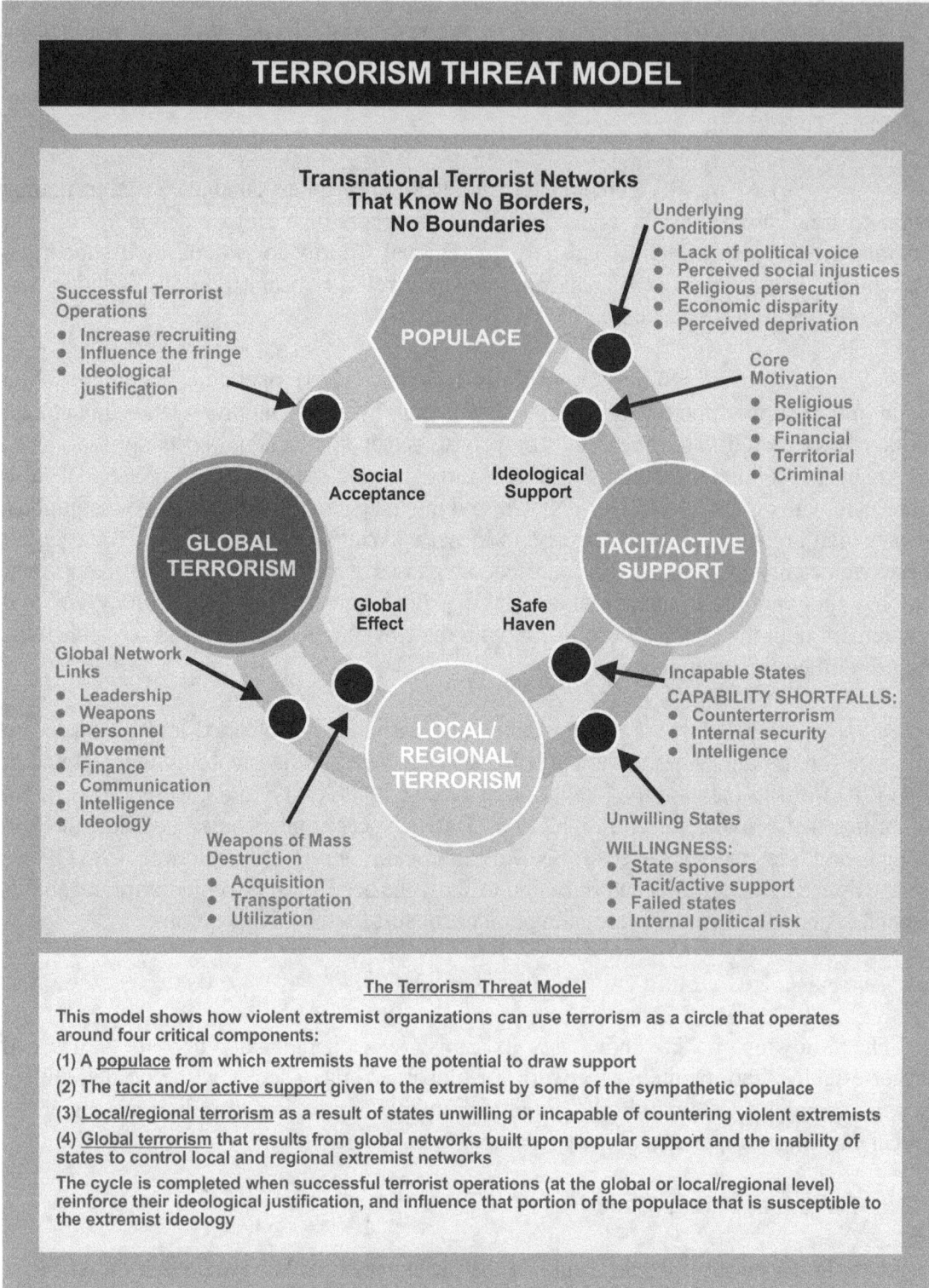

Figure III-2. Terrorism Threat Model

(2) It is the combination of the global network links and the VEOs' ability to generate global effects through terrorism (including the threat of their acquiring WMD) that pose the greatest strategic threat to the United States and PNs. Each component of the circle is enabled by the interdependent support mechanisms as shown. **Extremists develop active support for a given cause by espousing a message or ideology which resonates within a targeted populace.** Tacit/active support for their cause results from some combination of fear, sympathy, or apathy among those not inclined to fully believe the extremist message. As a popular support base develops, extremists gain and expand their freedom of action within those states willing but incapable of enforcing the rule of law within their own territory, or within nation states that support terrorism, or are unwilling to act to deny terrorists freedom of action. **Establishing global network links through a combination of safe havens and freedom of action permits VEOs to create global effects through terrorism.** Finally, the circle is completed when successful operations by the terrorists serve to reinforce their ideology, and influence their target populace. Typically, this brings even more new recruits and resources to their cause. The circle is repeated over time as the VEOs strengthen their global networks. Too often, the VEOs gain such popularity in their safe haven areas through disinformation and their public relations that they even sway a percentage of the moderate public opinion in some free societies.

b. **Counterterrorism Model**

(1) Figure III-3 is a model based on the application of the indirect and direct approach LOOs from the strategic campaign framework (discussed in paragraph 2, above) against the circular model of the terrorism threats.

(2) The CT threat model depicts specific LOOs from both the direct and indirect approaches linked to each component of the threat circle in integrated action to create the desired CT effects. A successful threat circle develops, evolves, and strengthens over a period of years and it will take time to prevent further growth, weaken its components, isolate its parts by further elimination of terrorist support, and reduce terrorist freedom of action. These actions will ultimately reduce the terrorism threat to a level where the extremists can be eliminated.

5. **Roles of Conventional Forces and Special Operations Forces**

a. **CF and SOF each bring certain competencies to CT efforts.** CF and SOF skills and capabilities complement each other. The scope, intensity, and duration of each specific operation will dictate the missions to be accomplished and the JFCs must determine the right joint force mix to employ. CF and SOF each possess unique capabilities that can produce even greater warfighting potential for the JFCs when integrated into a holistic global CT campaign with numerous theater CT operations. Flexible command and control (C2), specific mission generation processes, clear mission approval levels, integration of all appropriate partners at the operational level, and tactical interdependence improves the CT effectiveness of both CF and SOF .

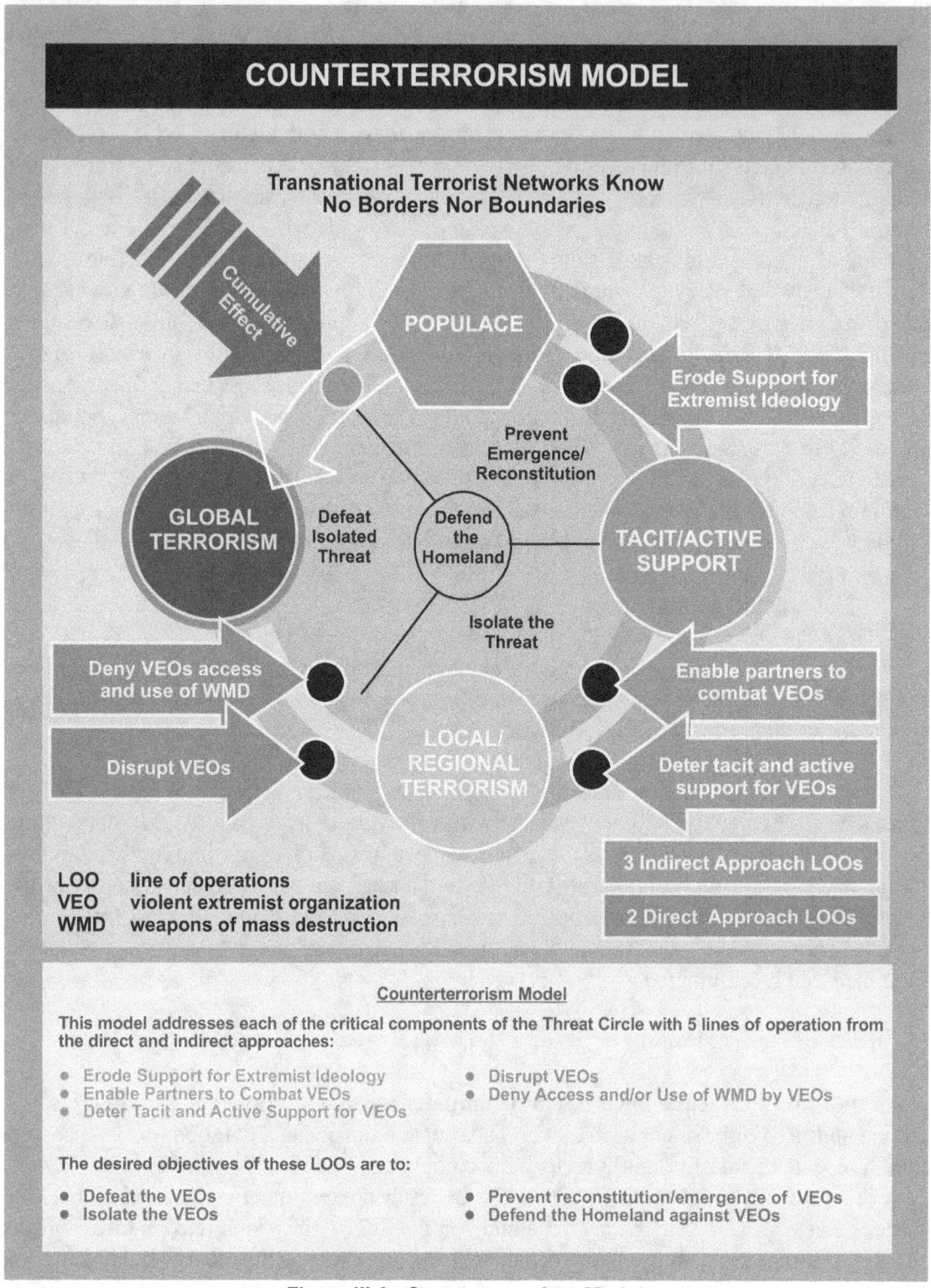

Figure III-3. Counterterrorism Model

**INTEGRATION OF CONVENTIONAL AND
SPECIAL OPERATIONS FORCES**

During Operation IRAQI FREEDOM, operations such as those resulting in deaths of the Hussein brothers and Abu Masab al-Zarqawi demonstrated the synergies that can be produced by integrating conventional forces and special operations forces.

From Multiple Sources

b. **CT is a core task of SOF, but global demand for CT activities and the varied conditions under which the broad range of CT activities occur dictates that SOF cannot be the sole force engaged in CT operations.** SOF generally perform two types of activities. First, they perform tasks that CF do not, and second, they perform tasks that can be done by the CF, but do so to a unique set of conditions and standards, normally using tactics, techniques, and procedures not used by CF. SOF perform nine specific core tasks as depicted below.

SPECIAL OPERATIONS FORCES CORE TASKS

-- Counterterrorism	-- Unconventional Warfare
-- Direct Action	-- Foreign Internal Defense
-- Special Reconnaissance	-- Information Operations
-- Counterproliferation of Weapons of Mass Destruction	-- Psychological Operations
	-- Civil Affairs Operations

Joint Publication 3-05, *Doctrine for Joint Special Operations*

NOTE: Commander, US Special Operations Command (CDRUSSOCOM) is responsible for synchronizing planning for global operations against terrorist networks and will do so in coordination with other combatant commands, the Services, and, as directed, appropriate USG agencies. As such, US Special Operations Command (USSOCOM) considers its role in the synchronization of DOD efforts to be a core task of its headquarters.

c. **Executing protracted CT operations will increasingly require CF to perform missions that traditionally have been viewed primarily as SOF activities.** CF personnel should receive cultural and language training for the operational areas to which they deploy. They should be capable of operating in smaller, more cross-functional units, under independent authorities and for prolonged periods. They should be able to plan, gather and disseminate intelligence/information and operate in coordination with interagency and multinational partners. Increased CF interaction abroad is an opportunity to gain area familiarization and gather useful information about potential operational areas. Employment of CF in efforts to build the capacity of PNs serves both to improve the capability of the CF in CT operations as well as develop those capabilities in our partners.

(1) **CF role in CT operations.** The focus on the population leads to the need for a number of small units operating throughout a potentially large operational area. These units may be operating in conjunction with the forces of other PNs, as trainers or advisors, or they may be operating independently. In any case, the CF may be required to provide combat support; combat service support (CSS), and sustainment. Specific examples of CF support to CT include, but are not limited to:

(a) Delivering precision fires and providing ISR to forces conducting CT operations throughout an operational area.

(b) Conducting preemptive attacks on terrorist targets, as directed by the JFC.

(c) Providing combat support and sustainment to multiple small, dispersed teams in permissive or hostile operational areas.

(d) Providing emergency extraction and personnel recovery for all joint forces in an operational area.

(e) Establishing security for OGAs or PNs that support CT operations.

(f) Operating in a support relationship to the dedicated US or PN CT forces and conducting strikes, raids, and other combat operations against terrorist training camps, safe havens, and other targets when the precision-strike capabilities of dedicated CT forces are not required to perform the mission.

(g) Support WMD elimination operations.

(2) **Building PN security force capacity in operational areas on a global scale.** The CF possess the basic skills necessary to train and advise indigenous forces in basic military skills in order to enhance the internal security of PNs vulnerable to terrorism. CF units normally will require specific assets be made available to equip indigenous forces. To do this effectively, the CF require language and cultural instruction, equipment, and other support necessary to train and advise indigenous forces in CT operations. CF may be required to provide a safe-haven for friendly armed groups that will allow them to establish either literal or virtual centers to publicize their cause, conduct recruitment, solicit funding, and/or serve as a venue for SC efforts.

(3) **Providing CMO activities such as interim military government or performing civil administration functions.** Like SOF, CF may be required to establish an interim military government or perform civil administration functions for stability operations in occupied or liberated territory when indigenous institutions, IGOs, or OGAs cannot do so. Failure to rapidly establish or reestablish order and basic services will encourage terrorist recruitment and support for their causes. This may require additional capabilities for intelligence, counterintelligence, security, and law enforcement functions in support of population security and the development of good governance.

d. **Integrating CF and SOF – C2 requirements.** In general, support relationships provide the best framework for integrated CF/SOF operations. This relationship allows the supported commander to set requirements and allows the supporting commander the flexibility to determine methods and tactics. To fully integrate CF and SOF, effective liaison must be maintained with all components of a joint force that may impact the conduct of their activities. The use of a number of CF and SOF liaison and control elements will help ensure the proper coordination of missions, minimize potential for friction between the forces, and sustain unity of effort. Circumstances may dictate that SOF support CF; and conversely, that CF support SOF. Integration enables the JFC to take full advantage of CF and SOF core competencies. SOF are most effective when special operations are fully integrated into the overall plan and the execution of special operations is through proper SOF C2 elements responsive to the needs of the supported commander. SOF C2 elements are provided to the supported or the supporting CF commanders and include joint special operations task forces (JSOTFs) or combined JSOTFs when organized with multinational SOF to conduct specific special operations or special operations in support of a larger joint operation or theater campaign; special operations C2 elements to synchronize integrated SOF/CF operations; and special operations liaison elements to coordinate, deconflict, and integrate special operations air, surface, and subsurface operations with conventional air operations. The exchange of SOF and CF liaison officers is essential to enhance situational awareness and facilitate staff planning and training for integrated operations.

e. **Integrating CF and SOF - operational planning requirements.** When properly integrated during planning, CF and SOF can capitalize on their collective strengths to achieve the JFC's intent. Ignoring CF and SOF integration issues during planning may either increase risk or miss opportunities to integrate with other partners involved in the CT activities. Effective crisis response depends on gaining early warning of potential problems. CF and SOF missions with foreign military forces can provide early recognition of these areas. SOF are especially adept in providing cultural awareness and can help facilitate the introduction of CF into an area or region. Likewise, CF can enable the introduction and support of SOF into denied areas, providing them logistical bases of operations, fire support, and reinforcements.

For detailed discussion of integrating CF and SOF, see USSOCOM Publication 3-33, Conventional Forces and Special Operations Forces Integration and Interoperability Handbook and Checklist.

6. **Strategic and Operational Planning Considerations**

a. **Strategic Assumptions**

(1) **A long war.** The war on terrorism is a long-term war of varying intensity that can be expected to take decades of effort.

(2) **Violent extremists will use any means of attack.** The United States and other free and open societies will remain principal targets of the extremists. They may seek to use all means of attack, including WMD against targets at home and abroad.

(3) **Internal struggle within societies.** Extremists are waging a global war to gain control over their communities and freedom is seen as a primary obstacle to their success. Violent extremists are hostile to the United States and the other societies for philosophical, political, and other ideological reasons, but portray the religious aspect as the primary reason. The world, in general, has a large stake in the defeat of violent extremists. The al-Qaeda network is the best example of an immediate strategic threat to the United States, and our partners, and mainstream Muslims.

(4) **Ideology matters.** Violent extremist movements can make new terrorists faster than the GCTN partnership can directly eliminate them. Ideological support and propaganda operations are a foundation for extremist success and a key to their recruitment and indoctrination.

(5) **Enemies within friends.** The networks of terrorist groups and others who support their violent extremist ideologies will influence, and in some cases penetrate, the governmental, civil, and religious institutions of PNs.

(6) **Together and alone.** The United States prefers to operate in a partnership with other countries to combat violent extremism, but will act alone, as necessary.

(7) **All instruments of national power required.** The United States is at war, and success will require the coordinated efforts of all instruments of US and PN power. In fact, the principal thrust must come from instruments of national power and influence outside DOD. The United States will also promote freedom, democracy, and economic prosperity around the world to mitigate those conditions that terrorists seek to exploit.

(8) **Divided responsibilities.** Responsibilities for protecting the United States are divided among Federal, state, and local governments and the private sector. DOD will need to coordinate closely with OGAs to achieve integrated plans for unified action. A detailed understanding of this division of responsibility is necessary for developing operation/campaign plans. This division of responsibility is continuously evolving and should be reviewed throughout the planning process as well as during execution.

b. **Key Considerations**

(1) **Close neighbors.** To protect the homeland, cooperation with neighbors in this hemisphere is especially important.

(2) **Enemies are transnational.** Our enemies in the war on terrorism do not respect national boundaries. VEOs cooperate with opportunists — other extremists, criminal elements, proliferators, and drug cartels — based on self-interest. The USG will need to use its country teams abroad in new ways to execute a global strategy.

(3) **Common assessment of threat.** USG agencies will not automatically adopt a common assessment of the threat or a common understanding of the nature of the war; nor

will CT PNs. The challenge is pursuing the right efforts to gain greater commonality of view.

(4) **Networked enemy.** A "networked enemy" has certain vulnerabilities that can be exploited. Although some nodes of the network are difficult to see, others may be identified and acted upon. Perturbations of nodes in the network may present opportunities for intelligence collection and/or allow more effective exploitation. Networked enemies have different vulnerabilities than hierarchical enemies. There may be vulnerabilities especially in network links consisting of non-ideological opportunists.

c. **Operational Art.** Operational art is the application of creative imagination by commanders and staffs — supported by their skill, knowledge, and experience — to design strategies, campaigns, and major operations and organize and employ military forces. Operational art also promotes unified action by helping JFCs and their staffs understand how to facilitate the integration of other agencies and multinational partners toward achieving the national strategic end state. This should be part of the JFC's joint operation planning process, and it lends itself to CT operations, especially when CT is combined with other IW-type operations within an operational area.

d. **Operational Design.** Operational design is the conception and construction of the framework that underpins a campaign or major operation plan and its subsequent execution. Joint operation planning — particularly for extensive operations that require a campaign (e.g., global campaign against terrorism) — uses various elements of operational design to help commanders and staffs visualize the arrangement of joint capabilities in time, space, and purpose to accomplish the mission. **For integrating CF and SOF in CT operations, operational design, incorporating operational art, provides the necessary planning tool for bringing clarity of purpose and structure to that complex operational level planning.**

Refer to JP 5-0, Joint Operation Planning, *for a detailed discussion of the elements of operational design as well as the applications of operational art and design in planning joint operations.*

e. **Effects in Joint CT Operations.** Like all operations, CT operations create effects which must be considered in the context of long-term efforts. These operations contribute most to the global campaign when higher order effects are considered, and actions are oriented toward creating the effects necessary to degrade terrorist networks. See Figure III-4 for a depiction of the relationships of missions, objectives, effects, and tasks for the various command echelons.

(1) Influencing the relevant population. Because CT operations can be as much about "influencing relevant populations" as finding the terrorists themselves, successful CT operational planning analyzes both desired and potential undesired effects. This is so because when the focus is on the population, a tactical miscue can create one, or a set of, undesired effects and result in a significant strategic setback.

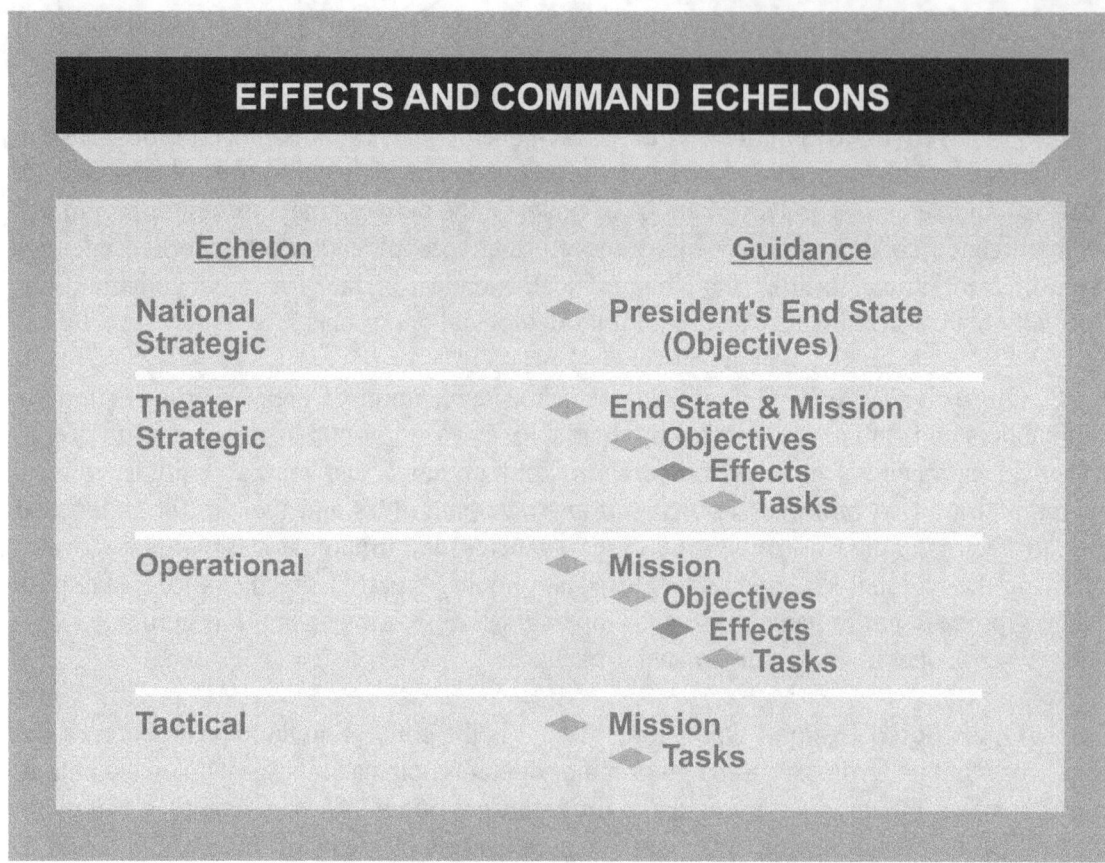

Figure III-4. Effects and Command Echelons

(2) Direct and indirect effects. **At the tactical level, a direct effect is the proximate, first-order consequence of an action** — for example, the elimination of a "wanted" terrorist by a precision attack, or restoration of electrical power to a relevant area by military engineers after a terrorist attack. Direct effects are most evident against structural systems. Indirect effects often are less observable or recognizable than direct effects, particularly when they involve changes in an adversary's behavior. However, an indirect effect often is the one more desired, such as the aforementioned change in the adversary's behavior — which may lead to adversary operational vulnerabilities that can then be exploited, such as the exposure and capture of a high-value individual (HVI).

> *Objectives* prescribe friendly goals.
>
> *Effects* describe system behavior in the operational environment — *desired effects are the conditions related to achieving objectives*.
>
> *Tasks* direct friendly action.
>
> **Joint Publication 5-0, Joint Operation Planning**

Refer to JP 5-0, Joint Operation Planning, *for further details about the use of effects as an element of operational design.*

CHAPTER IV
COMMAND AND CONTROL

> *"Never tell people how to do things. Tell them what to do and they will surprise you with their ingenuity."*
>
> **General George S. Patton**

1. General

Rarely in history have the effects of tactical level actions been so pronounced at the national strategic level as during the large scale CT and COIN operations in Iraq and Afghanistan. This realization has been fully recognized by the national level authorities and down the chain of command to the warfighters. Effectively countering terrorism may require more complex C2 and interagency coordination. This chapter outlines the roles, responsibilities, and authorities of some of the individuals and organizations at the national strategic and operational levels that exercise C2, interagency coordination, or otherwise influence unified action against terrorism worldwide. Additionally, multinational planning considerations are briefly addressed.

2. National Level

a. **President and Secretary of Defense.** The President is responsible for national strategic direction. When the President directs that CT operations be conducted, the Armed Forces of the United States provide the military instrument of national power. Ideally, the military instrument is used as a last resort, but should always be used in concert with the other instruments of national power: diplomatic, informational, and economic. SecDef is responsible to the President for creating, supporting, and employing military capabilities, to include CT military capabilities. Presidential directives guide participation by all USG departments and agencies for unified action for such operations.

b. **National Security Council (NSC).** The NSC is the principal forum for consideration of national security policy requiring Presidential determination. Of high importance among these policy determinations are the national security implications of terrorism and CT. The NSC advises and assists the President in integrating all aspects of national security policy. Along with its subordinate committees, the NSC is the principal means for coordinating, developing, and implementing national security policy.

c. **National Counterterrorism Center (NCTC)**

(1) The NCTC is the primary organization in the USG for integrating and analyzing all intelligence possessed or acquired pertaining to terrorism (except purely domestic terrorism). It provides all-source intelligence support to government-wide CT activities; establishes its own information technology systems and architectures, and those between the NCTC and other agencies.

(2) The NCTC serves as the principal advisor to the Director of National Intelligence (DNI) on intelligence operations and analysis relating to CT.

(3) **Unique among US agencies, the NCTC also serves as the primary organization for strategic operation planning for CT.** Operating under the policy direction of the President, the NSC, and the Homeland Security Council (HSC), the NCTC provides a full-time interagency forum and process to plan, integrate, assign lead operational roles and responsibilities, and measure the effectiveness of strategic-level CT activities of the USG. It is responsible for the integration of all instruments of national power to the CT mission.

d. **USG Participation in Domestic CT**

(1) **Homeland Security Council.** The HSC provides a parallel forum to the NSC for considering unique homeland security matters, especially those concerning terrorism within the homeland. The HSC is responsible for advising and assisting the President with respect to all aspects of homeland security and serves as the mechanism for ensuring coordination of homeland security related activities of executive departments and agencies, as well as the effective development and implementation of homeland security policies.

(2) **Department of Homeland Security (DHS).** DHS leads the unified national effort to secure the US. Key among its strategic goals is to prevent, protect, respond, and recover from acts of terrorism.

(3) **United States Northern Command (USNORTHCOM).** For threats or acts of terrorism within the USNORTHCOM AOR, the Department of Justice (DOJ) is the primary agency within US territory, and DOS is the primary agency on foreign territory. At the direction of the President or SecDef, Commander, USNORTHCOM (CDRUSNORTHCOM) may be directed to support the primary agency for CT operations in accordance with appropriate laws and regulations. To enable CT activities, timely intelligence and data exchange is conducted between the North American Aerospace Defense Command (NORAD), USNORTHCOM and other partners, to include multinational, local, state, tribal and federal entities. Partnering with the NCTC and the Defense Intelligence Agency's Joint Intelligence Task Force — Combating Terrorism (JITF-CT) and participating in the Bilateral Consultative Group on Counterterrorism (a mechanism used by the US and Canada to work on important bilateral issues and includes representatives of DOS, Federal Bureau of Investigation (FBI), NSC, DOJ, DHS and Canadian counterparts), NORAD and USNORTHCOM have access to many sources of intelligence, information and data to support the NORAD and USNORTHCOM missions and provide mutual support to other agencies engaged in combating terrorism. Military CT operations within the AOR would typically be the responsibility of CDRUSNORTHCOM.

For more information on USG departments and interagency coordination in the homeland see JP 3-27, Homeland Defense, *and JP 3-28,* Civil Support.

3. United States Special Operations Command

CDRUSSOCOM is a global synchronizer for the war on terrorism and responsible for synchronizing planning, and as directed, executing operations against terrorist networks on a global basis in coordination with other combatant commands, the Services, and as directed, appropriate USG agencies.

a. **Authority to Synchronize Efforts.** CDRUSSOCOM has the authority to synchronize and lead a collaborative planning process leveraging other combatant command capabilities and expertise that results in decentralized execution by both USSOCOM and other combatant commands against terrorist networks designated by the SecDef. The USSOCOM Center for Special Operations (CSO) is the fusion point for DOD synchronization efforts, combining operations, intelligence, and long-range planning and strategy.

b. **CDRUSSOCOM Responsibilities:**

(1) Integrating DOD CT strategy into plans, establishing intelligence priorities, and leading the development and synchronization of plans for operations against designated terrorist networks as part of a DOD global campaign plan.

(2) Prioritizing and synchronizing those parts of security cooperation activities, deployments, and capabilities that support campaigns against terrorist networks in coordination with GCCs.

(3) Executing C2 of CT operations, as directed.

(4) Providing representation, in addition to other military commands, to US national and international agencies for matters related to US and multinational operations against terrorist networks.

(5) Planning operational preparation of the environment (OPE), and as directed, executing OPE or synchronizing the execution of OPE in coordination with GCCs.

(6) Supporting other combatant commanders (CCDRs) for operational planning as required against terrorist network targets.

(7) Developing and leading a time sensitive planning process to rapidly propose courses of action (COAs) and to provide operational recommendations to SecDef or the President considering the full range of military options.

(8) Interfacing with national, Service, and commercial laboratories to maintain awareness of promising state of the art technology for the warfighter.

(9) Leading the development of a war on terrorism intelligence campaign plan for DOD.

4. Other Combatant Commands

Commanders of combatant commands exercise combatant command (command authority) (COCOM) over assigned forces and are responsible to the President and SecDef for the performance of assigned missions and the preparedness of their commands to perform assigned missions. For the war on terrorism, typically a GCC is the supported CCDR with the CDRUSSOCOM supporting. However, for specific missions as may be directed by the President or SecDef, CDRUSSOCOM may be the supported CCDR with the GCC(s) supporting in their AOR(s).

a. **Retain Control of AOR for CT Operations.** GCCs retain control of their AORs and COCOM of their assigned forces and operational control (OPCON) of attached forces. The primary role of CDRUSSOCOM is to synchronize CT operations and activities at the strategic level and arrange military actions to ensure the optimum employment of forces for CT. This synchronization facilitates unified action and allows USSOCOM to look "between the seams" as terrorists move, communicate, finance their activities, and operate around the world.

b. **Supported Command within Theater.** The GCCs have the best regional focus and knowledge of the operational environment in their AORs. They continue to execute operations, including CT missions, as the supported commanders in their respective theaters, with CDRUSSOCOM in a supporting role unless directed otherwise by the President or SecDef.

(1) To provide the necessary unity of command, GCCs are normally authorized a theater special operations command (TSOC) — a subunified command which serves as the primary organization by which the GCC exercises C2 over SOF. The TSOC also serves as a joint force special operations (SO) component command equivalent to a Service component command under the GCC. TSOCs ensure SOF are fully integrated into a GCC's collective security plans, contingency operations, and are focused on planning and conducting joint SO, to include CT operations, ensuring that SOF capabilities are properly matched to mission requirements, and advising their GCC on the proper employment of SOF. Typically, the GCC has COCOM over assigned SOF and exercises it through the commander of the TSOC. For attached SOF, the GCC has OPCON, which is normally exercised by the commander of the TSOC or another JFC subordinate to the GCC (e.g., commander, JSOTF [CDRJSOTF]); commander, joint PSYOP task force; or commander, joint CMO task force). The TSOC commander normally coordinates any operational links and command relationships between SOF and CF for approval by the appropriate JFC.

(2) The GCC has COCOM of assigned conventional forces and OPCON of attached forces, and exercises these authorities through the respective Service component commanders or functional component commanders. The appropriate component commanders normally discuss and then recommend for the JFC approval, the preferred command relationships, between conventional units and SOF.

(3) Integrated SOF and CF operations are typically conducted under the OPCON of a subordinate JFC with SOF and conventional units in support or tactical control (TACON) relationships.

c. **Prepare Supporting Campaign Plans.** The GCCs prepare theater campaign/operation plans that support the DOD global campaign plan against terrorism. These plans provide broad strategic concept of operations (CONOPS) and sustainment for achieving multinational, national, and theater strategic objectives. These plans enable USSOCOM to synchronize the interdependent, cross-AOR, missions for CT.

Refer to JP 1, Doctrine for the Armed Forces of the United States, *for detailed discussion of responsibilities of CCDRs or command relationships.*

5.   **Joint Task Force Considerations**

a. The C2 requirements for a joint task force (JTF) for CT operations are largely dependent upon its size, composition, organization, mission, the situation, and the size of the joint operations area (JOA). CT operations may be part of a larger IW-type situation (e.g., insurgency) for which the JFC is responsible. The GCC will designate a subordinate JFC and establish the JTF on a functional or geographic basis. The JFC normally will have OPCON of the JTF and exercise it through Service or functional component commanders. When integrating CF and SOF for joint operations, the JFC will typically establish support relationships, often with mission-type orders, or alternatively, some operations may require TACON as the command relationship. For some CT operations/tasks it may be advantageous for the JFC to use Service force components or SOF because their command lines are clear and uncomplicated. CT operations may be led by another interagency partner (e.g., US ambassador/DOS), and the JFC will be in support. The GCC normally will maintain coordination with an established US ambassador, or the appropriate DOS representative, and the JFC will have the appropriate interagency representatives/liaisons required for the tasked unified action.

b. For a given JOA within a GCC's AOR, the JFC responsible for CT operations will typically be a commander, joint task force (CJTF) (subordinate to the GCC) or a CDRJSOTF if predominately a SOF organization. CF/SOF Service force components normally are part of the JTF/JSOTF, respectively. Dependent upon the mission, the CJTF/CDRJSOTF could have a joint CMO task force and/or a joint PSYOP task force, or their equivalent task groups/elements, attached as components (or staff elements). If operations are conducted with HN, OGA, or multinational components, for unity of effort, their coordination relationships must be determined when the JFC organizes the force, and exchanging experienced liaison officers/personnel among the components is essential.

c. The JFC must establish operational areas within the JOA for the joint force and other components when continuing operations are expected. Procedures must be established for coordinating operations along/across operational boundaries within the JOA. The JFC should designate areas of operations (AOs) for the surface components and joint special operations area(s) (JSOAs) for the SOF, as required. CT operations are typically land-oriented, and within a land force commander's AO or a JSOA. The land force commander may subdivide the AO into smaller contiguous operational areas, and may assign units of the land forces (including multinational and HN components) responsibilities within those smaller operational areas as a matter of decentralized execution for operations. This decentralization of execution requires an efficient C2 system (organizational structure and communications architecture) at the component and tactical levels. Without robust C2 and combat identification capabilities, situational awareness of friendly and enemy force dispositions are difficult, because CT operations are normally nonlinear.

d. C2 for Joint Air Support of CT Operations. Some CJTFs may not have their own Air Force component commander. In such situations, the CJTF may have to establish support relationships with the GCC's Air Force component commander. The C2 arrangements must be fully coordinated to allow for the decentralized execution of air support typically required for CT operations. A CDRJSOTF may have a joint special operations air component commander, but will likely need a support relationship with an Air Force component commander.

e. The JFC establishes control and coordination measures (including a geospatial reference system for the JOA) for maneuver and movement control, airspace coordination, fire support, restrictive areas, etc.

f. C2 is essential for targeting. Targeting supports the process of linking the JFC's desired effects of fires to actions and tasks at the component level. The JFC should anticipate that CT operations will result in numerous time-sensitive targets in the form of HVIs and other fleeting targets of opportunity. The JFC may find the bulk of CT targeting with the land component or SOF.

For detailed discussion of organizing a joint force, and establishing operational areas, command authorities, and command relationships refer to JP 3-0, Joint Operations. For a discussion of joint security areas, refer to JP 3-10, Joint Security Operations in Theater.

6. **Multinational Considerations**

In working with multinational partners, the success of CT operations hinges on the US ability to work within each partner's political restraints, traditional structures, policies, and procedures. This requirement includes a multinational partner's willingness to not only coordinate and operate with the US military but with OGAs as well. Once an accord is reached between the US military and its multinational partners, a more rapid sharing of CT intelligence, coordination, and synchronization of operation plans and orders, missions, and other related documents and information can occur.

a. **C2 of US Forces in Multinational CT Operations.** Multinational CT command structures follow the same premise as for other multinational operations.

(1) Overview. Nations will rarely relinquish national command of their forces. As Commander in Chief, the President always retains and cannot relinquish national command authority over US forces.

(a) Command authority for a multinational force commander normally is negotiated between the participating nations and can vary from nation to nation. Command authority could range from OPCON, to TACON, to designated support relationships, to coordinating authority.

(b) While the President cannot relinquish national command authority, in some multinational environments it might be prudent or advantageous to place appropriate US forces under the OPCON of a foreign commander to achieve specified military objectives.

(c) In many cases, coordinating authority may be the only acceptable means of accomplishing a multinational mission. **Coordinating authority** is a consultation relationship between commanders, not an authority by which C2 may be exercised.

(2) Multinational CT Task Force. Within a larger military organizational structure, a multinational CT task force may be established to conduct operations that can better coordinate and synchronize the multifaceted CT capabilities of multinational partners, the interagency, regional and multilateral organizations, and various other countries' organizations (e.g., intelligence organizations, law enforcement organizations). There should be sufficient flexibility within the task force whereas one nation may be identified as the lead nation for a particular CT operation. This may occur because of sensitive political concerns with the method of sharing information, the relationship between countries, or a country's expertise.

b. **Operational Considerations**

(1) Strategic implications of all actions must be considered because of the nature of CT operations and competing multinational interests (e.g., political interests).

(2) Multinational partners must have a common goal and willingness to conduct CT operations.

(3) In CT operations, multinational partners must be willing to share information and synchronize other operational capabilities to ensure all available and required support is accessible. This equates to developing resilient, lasting, and collaborative relationships to use shared resources and expertise to counter terrorism.

(4) Multinational forces participation in CT exercises and operations builds vital relationships that influence cooperation, coordination, trust, and confidence in the fight against terrorism.

(5) Multinational forces must be treated as legitimate partners with appropriate trust and confidence.

(6) Under bilateral relationships, sensitivity is required to ensure third party countries are not offended, especially while working in combined facilities, such as in operations and intelligence planning, coordination, and execution.

For a detailed discussion regarding multinational force operations, refer to JP 3-16, Multinational Operations.

7. Interagency Coordination

> *"Many Global War on Terrorism [GWOT] activities are not limited to the Department of Defense. In fact, most GWOT tasks require actions by other government agencies and international partners."*
>
> **United State Special Operations Command Posture Statement 2007**

Within the context of DOD involvement, interagency coordination is the coordination that occurs between elements of DOD, and engaged USG agencies for the purpose of achieving an objective. The strategic security environment that is characterized by regional instability, failed states, increased weapons proliferation, transnational terrorism, and unconventional threats to US citizens, interests, and territories, requires even greater cooperation among interagency partners. In addition to military power, national CT strategic objectives require the coordinated use of the diplomatic, informational, and economic instruments of national power and other national capabilities that can only be accomplished through interagency coordination. The war on terrorism, and particularly the significant ongoing CT operations in various countries, has solidified the importance and necessity for effective and detailed interagency coordination not only at the national level, but down to the operational and tactical levels. **Continued success in CT operations demands an end to unilateral "stove piping" of action within departments, agencies, and staff directorates**. In a parallel context, **IGO and NGO coordination** refers to coordination among DOD elements and IGOs (including regional security organizations) and NGOs to achieve a mutual objective.

a. **Interagency Unity of Effort.** Success in the war against terrorism requires interagency coordination to maximize the effectiveness of all instruments of national power. USSOCOM, as the integrating command for global CT planning efforts, supports a growing network of relationships through continuous liaison partnerships, a supporting technical infrastructure, and using information sharing policies. Along with the interagency partners, this network draws upon an increasing number of countries, regional organizations, IGOs, NGOs, and the private sector to achieve unified action.

(1) Typically, each agency develops its own agency-specific plans at varying levels of detail in response to an issue, incident, or event. **The challenge to the interagency community with respect to CT operations is to meld the individual agency**

planning efforts into a collaborative, multi-agency planning process that exploits the core competencies of all the interagency partners.

(2) To enhance interagency coordination at the strategic and operational levels, joint interagency coordination groups (JIACGs) have been established at the GCCs. Additionally, USSOCOM has established an interagency task force to enhance operational effectiveness in the long war against terrorism and synchronize the interagency efforts of other combatant commands and designated joint forces commands.

b. **Joint Interagency Coordination Group.** Representing USG agencies at the combatant command headquarters, the JIACG is the CCDR's lead organization for interagency coordination providing guidance, facilitation, coordination, and synchronization of interagency activities within the AOR. The JIACG is an interagency staff group that establishes regular, timely, and collaborative working relationships between the USG civilian and military operational planners. In particular, the JIACG participates in security cooperation, contingency, crisis, and transition planning and facilitates information sharing across the interagency community.

(1) **Combatant Command Staff and the JIACG**

(a) Within the staff, the JIACG can provide the greatest value-added when authorized to coordinate across a CCDR's staff and with the components. Normally, the JIACG operates most effectively as a separate staff element reporting directly to the deputy CCDR or the chief of staff.

(b) A CT planning effort and subsequent operations may require a combatant command to request additional CT expertise from various agencies and organizations (e.g., Central Intelligence Agency, Defense Intelligence Agency, FBI, and National Security Agency) to staff its JIACG and optimize interagency effectiveness and efficiency. This arrangement also facilitates the use of reachback and collaboration between subordinate JFCs and the CCDR.

(2) **JIACG Participation in CT Exercises and Training Events.** Combatant commands, their subordinate JTFs, and interagency representatives (versus role players) should participate in CT related exercises and training events to build more viable working relationships, improve interoperability, and make use of lessons learned from real-world operations.

For more details concerning the JIACG, refer to JP 1, Doctrine for the Armed Forces of the United States, *JP 3-08,* Interorganizational Coordination During Joint Operations, *and the US Joint Forces Command Joint Warfighting Center,* Commander's Handbook for the Joint Interagency Coordination Group.

c. **USSOCOM Interagency Task Force.** This task force is a dedicated operations and intelligence planning team comprised of interagency intelligence and operations planning specialists and a robust information collection capability. All of the major interagency partners are represented in the task force to include the DOD combat support agencies (CSAs).

(1) The interagency task force searches for and identifies new, developing, and emerging CT opportunities to attack terrorist organizations and networks worldwide. It further develops actionable intelligence into operational COAs and plans against the emerging targets.

(2) Throughout this process, the interagency and CSA liaison partners provide the direct conduit for the flow of operational information and intelligence between their parent organizations and USSOCOM as the global CT synchronizer.

d. **Interagency Coordination Planning Considerations**

(1) CT operations require participation of all essential military and interagency planners.

(2) During the planning process it is crucial to understand who has the lead for a particular CT task.

(3) The prudent sharing of information is paramount to success. "Read in" other interagency partners that may not have direct participation in initial CT operations but may be required for subsequent operations.

(4) Consider the involvement of other stakeholders (e.g., IGOs, NGOs, and the private sector) in CT operations planning.

(5) At the subordinate joint force level (e.g., JTF), effective use of reachback to the combatant command JIACG and USSOCOM interagency task force is an invaluable resource. The ability of the various JIACG and interagency task force agencies to react quickly to requests for information can enhance branch and sequel development.

(6) Combatant commands' JIACGs should coordinate their CT planning with the USSOCOM interagency task force as appropriate.

CHAPTER V
SIGNIFICANT ENABLING FUNCTIONS FOR COUNTERTERRORISM

> *"…the terrorists and their supporters declared war on the United States. And war is what they got."*
>
> **President George W. Bush**
> **1 May 2003**

1. General

This chapter discusses specific enabling functions that are essential to all joint operations, but require special emphasis for CT operations.

2. Intelligence

In the aftermath of the September 11, 2001 terrorist attacks, the USG enhanced CT intelligence architecture and interagency collaboration by setting clear national priorities and transforming the organizational structure of the intelligence agencies to achieve those priorities. **The intelligence community (IC) has been reorganized and the DNI now oversees the IC to better integrate its efforts into a more unified, coordinated, and effective body.** The President established a mission manager organization, the NCTC, dedicated solely to planning and conducting intelligence operations against terrorist networks. The DNI launched an Open Source Center to coordinate open source intelligence and ensure this information is integrated into IC products. The FBI is fully integrated with the IC and has refocused its efforts on preventing terrorism. The Central Intelligence Agency has transformed to fulfill its role to provide overall direction and coordination for overseas human intelligence operations of IC elements. To undercut the financial underpinnings of terrorism worldwide, the Department of the Treasury created the Office of Terrorism and Financial Intelligence. The Defense Intelligence Operations Coordination Center (DIOCC) is the lead DOD intelligence organization responsible for integrating and synchronizing military intelligence and national intelligence capabilities in support of the combatant commands. **The USSOCOM CSO is the fusion point for DOD synchronization of CT plans and establishing intelligence priorities against terrorist networks.** The CSO provides a venue for regular meetings, briefings, and conferences with interagency members (including the GCCs) and PNs and provides a forum for consistent dialogue for ongoing planning and situational understanding that simply had not existed earlier. The continuous collaboration is augmented with a USSOCOM sponsored semiannual Global Synchronization Conference. The following discussion provides insight **as to the complexities and rigorous analyses involved in establishing requirements and obtaining the intelligence products required for CT**.

a. **Intelligence for Counterterrorism.** Accurate and timely intelligence is absolutely critical to CbT. All disciplines of intelligence are required for CT: human, imagery, signals, measurement and signature, technical, open source, and counterintelligence. Because of its global application, intelligence for CT is discussed in detail in the USSOCOM Concept

Plan 7500, *DOD Global War on Terrorism Campaign Plan*, Annex B - Intelligence (hereafter referred to as Annex B). It provides the combatant commands and the IC with a detailed common intelligence framework to support prosecution of the *DOD Global War on Terrorism Campaign Plan.*

   b. **Concept of Counterterrorism Intelligence Operations.** The concept of intelligence operations for CT developed in Annex B closely parallels the CONOPS for that campaign plan. It recognizes that intelligence requirements for global and regional operations against the primary enemy, the transnational terrorists (i.e., al-Qaeda), must also be synchronized with the intelligence requirements for regional operations (i.e., within AORs) against the secondary enemy, VEOs.

      (1) Intelligence processes and procedures for integration and synchronization include:

         (a) Assigning intelligence missions, roles, and responsibilities for the supporting, integrating, and synchronizing of the campaign plan.

         (b) Integrating national, theater, and PN intelligence plans.

         (c) Describing the integrated intelligence architecture to facilitate a common intelligence picture.

         (d) Developing priority intelligence requirements and intelligence tasks (for inclusion in the appropriate appendix to annex B (Intelligence), and a common counterterrorism analytical framework (CTAF) to understand the global CT threat and the operational environment.

         (e) Identifying collection and analysis and production (A&P) requirements, intelligence gaps, and the mitigation responsibilities for addressing the gaps.

         (f) Assessing and developing multinational intelligence capabilities to partner with the United States to defeat, disrupt and defend against terrorism.

         (g) Identifying doctrine, organization, training, material, leadership and education, personnel, and facilities shortfalls and mitigation responsibilities.

      (2) Assignment of Intelligence Task Lists. Specific intelligence task lists (ITLs) are developed for the specific intelligence requirements for each of the campaign LOOs. The ITL items drive the development of the national intelligence support plan (NISP) and the functional intelligence support plans which delineate capabilities required of the CSAs and Service intelligence centers to support the CT intelligence processes.

      (3) Collection. Annex B establishes processes and procedures to collaborate with US Strategic Command (USSTRATCOM) Joint Functional Component Command for Intelligence, Surveillance, and Reconnaissance (JFCC-ISR), Defense Intelligence Agency,

the combatant commands, and the other CSAs, to synchronize/deconflict CT collection requirements. USSOCOM reviews, evaluates and scores the GCC requirements for the JFCC-ISR allocation process, and uses the ITL matrices to assess collection capacity and identify shortfalls.

(4) A&P. Annex B identifies intelligence requirements which are the basis for intelligence production. **Production will focus on identifying the functions and resources terrorist groups need to operate.** The CTAF will be the model used as a guide to develop dynamic threat assessments (DTAs) for various terrorist groups (see Figure V-1). These DTAs will include designation of critical nodes, critical capabilities, critical requirements, and critical vulnerabilities.

(5) Intelligence Support for Regional (i.e., AOR) Operations Objectives. There are four types of intelligence analysis normally used in concert to ensure all aspects of the requirements are covered for regional operations and the global campaign.

(a) Geographic Analysis. This is traditional analysis with one exception: it is divided into transnational and regional analysis. **The JITF-CT is the primary A&P organization for transnational CT analysis, and the GCCs are the primary A&P organizations for regional CT analysis (within their AORs).**

(b) Relational Analysis. This analysis examines organizations, social networks, and transactions to identify the HVIs, critical requirements, and the relationships between people, functions, and the physical terrain/human environment.

(c) Geospatial and Cultural Analysis. This analysis combines geography with social science to predict where terrorists are operating or will operate. A multilayer analysis is the primary analytical output. Additionally, analyses of environmental and cultural data support this type of analysis.

c. **Global Campaign and Regional/Theater Operations Interface.** The GCCs develop plans for CT within their AORs and in support of the global campaign. The annex B (Intelligence) of their plans must be synchronized with Annex B. The GCCs ITLs also must support the global campaign LOOs. While USSOCOM ensures global campaign seams are covered, the GCCs also must identify known regional seams (e.g., between operational areas and AORs) and work with the other combatant commands to ensure coverage. Synchronization requires information sharing among the GCCs and USSOCOM. **GCCs have responsibility for intelligence A&P on all terrorist groups whose primary operating bases reside within their theater** (specific terrorist groups are designated during the federation process of intelligence planning).

d. **Actionable Intelligence.** Combatant commands require actionable intelligence, and that requirement is very relevant for CT operations from the strategic to the lowest tactical levels. Key elements of actionable intelligence are:

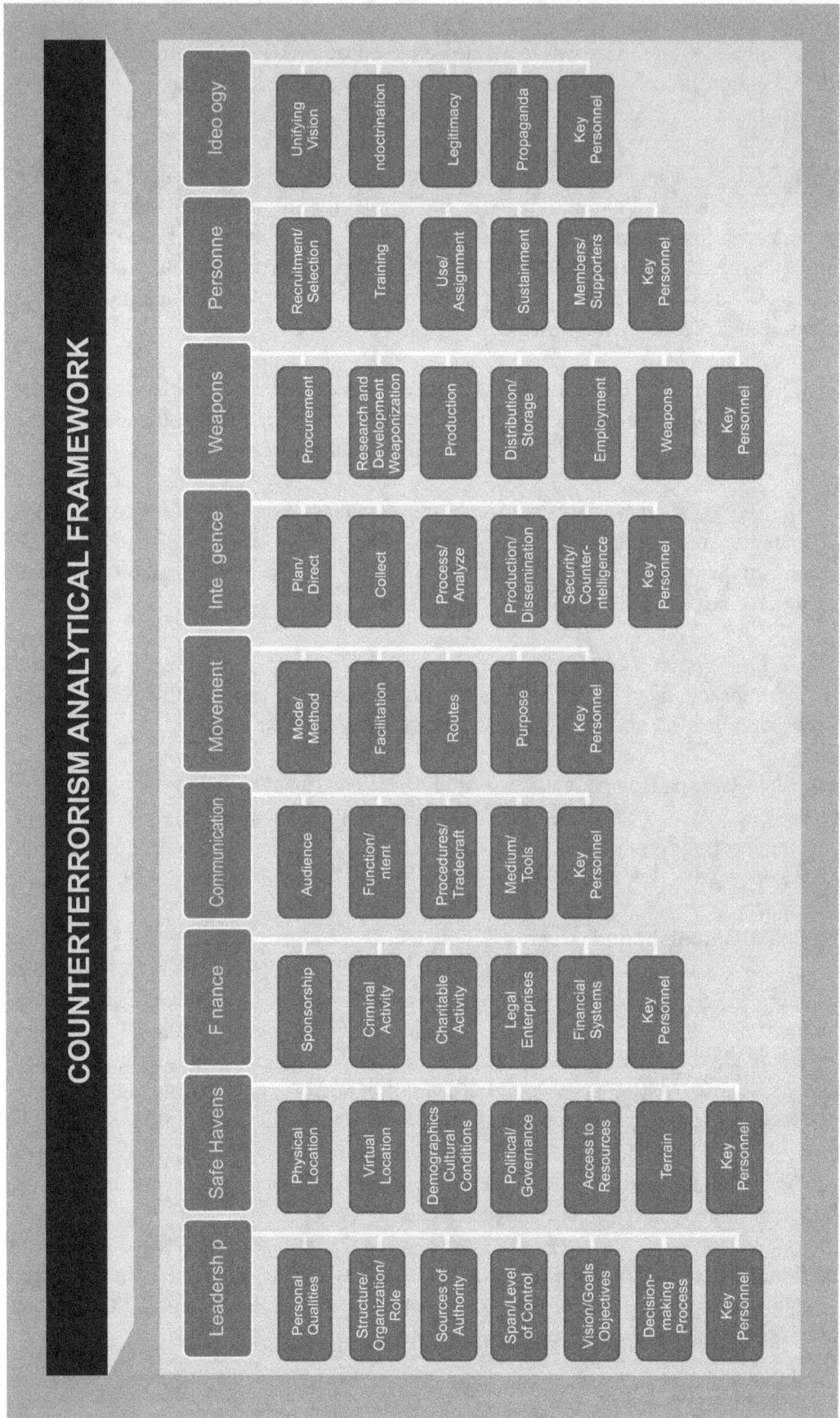

Figure V-1. Counterterrorism Analytical Framework

(1) **Location.** Providing an ellipse radius or "vicinity of" location, if possible. Even a probable location is worthwhile.

(2) **Facilities.** Providing useful data that can help identify the place when an HVI is involved, or where terrorist assets are located.

(3) **Time.** Providing the time of a sighting or an event. Time, as with location, helps to establish patterns that are exploitable. Time is also useful in establishing potential evidence that may link an HVI to actual or planned terrorist events.

(4) **Travel.** Providing information regarding movement and means of travel and other available details when they relate to HVIs.

(5) **Relationships/connections.** Providing known or suspected family/tribal relationships that exhibit or have potential for greater trust. CTAF functional **connections** show possible linkages from COG/critical capabilities to critical vulnerabilities.

e. **CTAF and COG-to-Critical Vulnerability Analysis.** The CTAF is used for DTAs that should include the COG-to-critical vulnerability analysis for a given VEO or terrorist group. It is important to understand that each terrorist group is different and what is deemed a COG for one may not apply to another and, on a case-by-case basis, use of the CTAF is key to the functional and resource analysis for determining their critical vulnerabilities. **Actionable intelligence on a terrorist group's critical vulnerabilities will provide a significant advantage in seizing the initiative.**

(1) **The CTAF and its nine categories** include the potential COGs or critical capabilities and **can provide a useful step towards a systems perspective of a terrorist group**. It is not intended as a static, linear, exclusive construct and should be modified as deemed necessary. It was designed as a guideline and developed as part of the common intelligence framework supporting all aspects of the *DOD Global War on Terrorism Campaign Plan*. While CTAF component functions and systems can appear interdependent or mutually exclusive of each other, they are interrelated through a series of simple or complex nodal relationships. **The exact nature of those relationships are identified and defined during the target system or network analysis** and the process requires timely, focused data on enemy functions and processes.

(2) The Annex B federation process establishes responsibilities for A&P of the CTAF for designated terrorist groups to drive intelligence operations and identify critical vulnerabilities using the critical factors methodology. Briefly stated, collection and analysis in support of the CTAF identifies the terrorist groups' COG/critical capabilities (normally CTAF subgroups) and then GCC and JITF-CT analysts determine the critical requirements needed to meet those critical capabilities, and which of those requirements are vulnerable to friendly action (making them critical vulnerabilities). A critical vulnerability level of understanding (i.e., actionable intelligence about Group X) is the level of detail needed to

act (disrupt, contain, isolate, neutralize, block, and interdict) against a designated terrorist group.

(3) The results of this analysis will appear in the DTAs and, as appropriate, in time critical reporting and planning. This process will drive the collection and production of the intelligence, and for time critical operations, may include dynamic re-tasking of collection assets and planning/targeting analysis.

(4) CTAF categories/components (Figure V-1) are as follows:

(a) **Leadership.** The direction of terrorist activities by individuals, organizations, and processes.

(b) **Safe havens.** The exploitation of an environment by terrorists to pursue their activities relatively free from detection and disruption.

(c) **Finance.** The generation, storage, movement, and use of assets to fund terrorist activities.

(d) **Communications.** The transferring of information in support of terrorist activities.

(e) **Movement.** The transferring of people and materials in support of terrorist activities.

(f) **Intelligence.** The collection, protection, and use of information to support terrorist activities.

(g) **Weapons.** The acquisition and employment of materials; to include WMD, and expertise to conduct terrorist attacks.

(h) **Personnel.** The acquisition and use of human assets in support of terrorist activities.

(i) **Ideology.** The interpretation and propagation of a shared belief system that motivates individuals to support terrorist activities.

Refer to USSOCOM Concept Plan 7500, DOD Global War on Terrorism Campaign Plan, Annex B – Intelligence, *for specific details regarding intelligence planning for the war on terrorism. Refer to JP 2-01,* Joint and National Intelligence Support to Military Operations, *for further doctrinal guidance regarding intelligence.*

3. Intelligence, Surveillance, and Reconnaissance

> ***intelligence, surveillance, and reconnaissance*** — *An activity that synchronizes and integrates the planning and operation of sensors, assets, and processing, exploitation, and dissemination systems in direct support of current and future operations. This is an integrated intelligence and operations function.*
>
> **Joint Publication 2-01,** *Joint and National Intelligence Support to Military Operations*

a. The Unified Command Plan assigns USSTRATCOM responsibility for global ISR. At the strategic level, JFCC-ISR collaborates with joint force providers and CCDRs to formulate and recommend allocation solutions to meet combatant command requirements for ISR resources, and ensures an integrated response for crisis-related and time-sensitive ISR requirements that cannot be satisfied by the supported CCDR's assigned or attached assets. DIOCC develops the ISR support plan located in the NISP that describes the processes used to prioritize, coordinate, and synchronize ISR for operations/campaigns like the *DOD Global War on Terrorism Campaign Plan.* USSOCOM, the GCCs, DIOCC, DNI, and JFCC-ISR coordinate and synchronize the ISR requirements and assets available to support the long war on terrorism.

b. At the strategic and operational levels, the JFC employs ISR forces assigned or attached to the joint force and requests support of national/interagency assets through a validation by the supported CCDR, normally a GCC. Some SOF unique requirements may be validated by CDRUSSOCOM in coordination with the appropriate GCCs.

c. Because **ISR is an integrated intelligence and operations function**, the joint force staff develops an overall collection strategy and posture for the execution of the ISR missions controlled by the JFC. The intelligence directorate of a joint staff, in coordination with the operations directorate of a joint staff, reviews, validates, and prioritizes all outstanding intelligence requirements for the JFC. The joint force air component commander (JFACC), if designated, provides integrated airborne ISR for the JFC. **The responsible JFC must properly prioritize ISR for CT among other operational needs.** The JFC may designate a joint collection management board to perform the ISR collection operations management, prioritization, and tasking functions.

d. **The JFACC normally is responsible for planning, coordinating, allocating, and tasking assigned airborne ISR assets to accomplish and fulfill JFC tasks and requirements.** ISR assets normally include manned and unmanned aircraft systems (UASs), some under the control of the JFACC, or made available by Service components to the JFACC for tasking. Many UASs and some aircraft are organic to, and remain under the control of their Service and SOF components. If assigned assets cannot fulfill specific airborne ISR requirements, the joint air operations center (JAOC) will request additional ISR support from the JFC or another joint force component, or the JFC requests support from the supported CCDR. It is imperative that the JFACC remains aware of all available airborne joint force ISR capabilities that can be used to support the JFC. SOF and the Service components may have organic assets that are not airborne nor dedicated to ISR, but capable of fulfilling an ISR requirement for the JFC. Those components should ensure the

JFC's ISR collection manager is also aware of the availability of their non-flying ISR capabilities.

e. National and non-DOD ISR resources normally are not placed under the OPCON of the JFC. Those resources may provide direct support to the JFC or one of the components, either full-time or on-call, but are normally shared with other commands, components or OGAs. The supported commander will be provided ISR liaison teams upon request. These teams will normally be the points of contact for coordinating their specific ISR resources and associated capabilities with the supported commander's ISR operators.

f. Normally, ISR personnel are integrated into the JAOC. The complexity of integrating airborne ISR will normally determine whether the function is handled by a specialty team, cell, or division within the JAOC. **The ISR collection managers and operations planners will work with the joint force staff and other components to effectively coordinate national and theater ISR objectives.**

g. As a land-centric mission, **CT may require more priority and a greater share of direct ISR support for tactical level land force commanders than for operational level decision makers** because of the nature of the threat and the enemy. For CT, time-sensitive targets are typically HVIs in urban environments, and tactical events frequently have strategic level effects, so the JFC must be able to properly balance where ISR support is aimed within the operational environment to be operationally effective.

4. **Logistics**

a. **General.** The war against terrorism requires robust logistic planning with global distribution requirements for the Services. The GCCs (and their Service component commands), can have significant distribution challenges as the components may have tactical units widespread across an operational area or an AOR. The designation of the support relationship for a CT plan/order is significant for logistic purposes. For long-term CT operations in specific operational areas, a GCC normally will be the supported CCDR and CDRUSSOCOM the supporting CCDR. If directed by SecDef, CDRUSSOCOM may be the supported CCDR and a GCC with the operational area in the AOR may be the supporting CCDR. Generally, for the purpose of this section the former is assumed, so the GCC will be the "supported CCDR" for CT operations. For CF in CT operations, it is unlikely CDRUSSOCOM would be logistically supporting those forces. The directive authority for logistics (DAFL) of both supported and supporting CCDRs necessitates a coordinated effort between them and among their Service component commands. CDRUSSOCOM has DAFL for SOF unique items.

b. **Assumptions and Planning Factors.** The following are significant and generally apply to CT operations, but may not for all.

(1) CT operations may receive priority over existing operations, and the transnational terrorist threat can require multiple CT operations within and across AORs.

Specific intertheater lift and material prioritization decisions will occur that ensure execution of priority CT operations.

(2) CDRUSSOCOM is generally responsible for the synchronization and coordination of logistics for SOF when executing across multiple AORs.

(3) Supporting GCCs will establish initial theater staging bases at designated locations, as required for deploying CT forces.

(4) Supporting GCCs will provide early access to aerial ports of embarkation (APOEs), seaports of embarkation, aerial ports of debarkation (APODs), seaports of debarkation (SPODs), and intermediate staging bases (ISBs). Alternate APODs and SPODs should be identified in anticipation of an area denial event such as a WMD attack and contamination or some other major force protection issues at the primary port.

(5) Supporting GCCs will coordinate host-nation support (HNS) and ensure HNS agreements established by the United States and PNs are in effect.

(6) Supporting GCCs will coordinate contract support.

(7) Supporting GCCs will ensure their Service component commanders provide common item and service unique support, and designate the lead Service for common user support within their AORs. Common support to other US services, interagency elements, and/or OGAs, PN, and multinational forces may be necessary.

(8) Lines of communications (LOCs) will remain open throughout operations.

(9) Supporting GCCs will focus on strategic and operational CSS, to include introducing C2 into the theater early, early entry CSS, and theater level distribution management. Deploying forces will include planning for combat support and CSS for bare-base locations.

(10) Supporting GCCs will phase operational logistics to coincide with operations, with initial logistic support inserted with operational forces.

(11) Supporting Service components will identify logistic shortfalls and limiting factors with their proposed resolutions to their GCC and the supported CCDR.

(12) Supporting GCCs may provide a joint deployment and distribution operations center (JDDOC) that will provide movement control, including trace, track, and expediting on proposed theater supply routes. The logistics directorate of a joint staff (J-4) at the combatant command will coordinate distribution requirements with the supporting JDDOC, which will in turn, coordinate with the US Transportation Command Deployment and Distribution Operations Center.

(13) Regional governments will provide base access (to include overflight rights), transit authority, and other PN support.

(14) CT plans/orders will set the number of days the deploying forces must be self sustaining.

(15) Supporting GCCs will coordinate additional logistic requirements with Service component commands, theater support activities, and national providers.

(16) Supporting GCCs will be prepared to provide operational logistics beyond combat operations; to include support to humanitarian assistance and disaster relief operations, and additional PSYOP and CA operations, as required by the operation plan/order.

(17) The supporting GCCs and CDRUSSOCOM will establish appropriate logistic coordination and reporting procedures between their staffs and among their Service component commands.

(18) The legal considerations of globally distributive logistic efforts for the war on terrorism requires that CCDRs involve a Judge Advocate or legal counsel in logistic planning, including their review of all supporting plans to ensure compliance with various international, US and HN laws, and applicable treaties, status-of-forces agreements, status of mission agreements, acquisition and cross-servicing agreements (ACSAs), memoranda of understanding, and memoranda of agreements.

(19) Logistic support agreements / contracts will provide the authority to obtain necessary logistic support from HN/PN. Established logistic support will be based on existing authorities and agreements (such as ACSAs), or newly obtained authorities and international agreements. All contracting support efforts will be conducted in accordance with all established regulatory guidance and directives.

c. **Concept of Logistic Support**

(1) Each supported CCDR should produce a logistic supportability analysis based on assigned/attached force structure, operational areas, and specific mission requirements for their CT operations. This analysis should consider the potential for a terrorist attack using WMD and operations in CBRN environments.

(2) Logistic support for US forces is fundamentally a Service responsibility (except USSOCOM for SOF unique items). Services will arrange for logistic support in accordance with current Service directives and the CCDR's plans/orders. The TSOC has responsibility for reception, staging, onward movement, and integration of all SOF in support of the GCC. USSOCOM coordinates through the GCC for SOF common sustainment and supply. Due to the short duration and high operating tempo of SO, deploying SOF provide a statement of requirements to the TSOC for coordination with the GCC's subordinate commands.

(3) CCDRs exercising their DAFL will plan for and establish administrative and logistic systems, including sustainment and distribution that most effectively support the globally distributed CT mission requirements.

(4) The United States and PNs are responsible for providing sufficient logistic and contracting capability necessary to provide any logistic support, supplies and/or services that are beyond the CCDRs capabilities. Whenever possible, ACSAs with eligible PNs, and cooperative security locations will be negotiated in advance so as to increase the flexibility and timeliness of mutual logistic support.

(5) Logistic distribution and allocation issues that cannot be resolved among/between Services and CCDRs should be forwarded to Joint Staff J-4 for consideration by the Joint Materiel Priorities and Allocation Board.

(6) If a warning order or execute order is issued pertaining to a concept or operation plan, a Chairman of the Joint Chiefs of Staff (CJCS) project code normally will be issued to expedite supply actions. However, this may increase visibility of an operation, so operations security must be considered prior to assigning any project code.

d. **Priorities.** The numerous CT operations around the globe, utilizing various elements of US and PN instruments of national power, require continuing assessment, and prioritization of actions/support. Some general statements of priorities affecting logistics include:

(1) Priority of Support: ISBs, APOE/APOD, build-up of sustainment, and LOCs.

(2) Priority of Sustainment: ammunition, fuel, food/water, and base support.

(3) Priority of Movement: deploying forces and sustainment.

(4) Priority of Engineer Effort: force protection, LOC, APOD, and SPOD maintenance.

Basic logistics policy and guidance are provided in JP 4-0, Joint Logistics, and Chairman of the Joint Chiefs of Staff Instruction (CJCSI) 3110.03, Logistics Supplement To The Joint Strategies Capabilities Plan (JSCP). Other specific logistic subject matter is contained in the other JP-series publications.

5. Legal

a. **Application of the Law of War.** Commanders at all levels ensure their forces operate in accordance with the "law of war," often called the "law of armed conflict." The law of war encompasses all international law for the conduct of hostilities binding on the United States or its individual citizens, including treaties and international law agreements to which the United States is a party, and applicable customary international law. It specifically applies to all cases of declared war or any other armed conflict between the United States and other nations; and by policy, the principles and spirit of the law of war applies to all military operations. With CT operations in numerous locations across the globe, **JFCs must be particularly aware of the status of their conflict, the legal basis for their use of force, the characterization of enemy combatants, civilians taking a direct part in the hostilities, and potential detainees**.

For further guidance on the law of war, refer to CJCSI 5810.01C, Implementation of the DOD Law of War Program. *For detailed information and guidance on legal support, refer to JP 1-04,* Legal Support to Military Operations.

b. **Legal Basis for Use of Force.** Nearly every military decision and action has potential legal considerations and implications. A legal basis must exist for every decision to use military force. In a general sense, under customary international law, as reflected in the United Nations Charter and elsewhere, the United States has the inherent right of self-defense against hostile acts or demonstrations of hostile intent toward the United States or its citizens, including the use of force in anticipatory self-defense. Additionally, US forces may be acting under a UNSCR to take action to restore international peace and security in a particular area. Actions within the sovereign territory of another state should be based on either the consent of that state, a UNSCR, or a Presidential determination that such is necessary either in response to an armed attack or in anticipation of an imminent armed attack. Normally, for a given operation, the JFC has approved rules of engagement (ROE)/rules for the use of force (RUF) that govern the use of military force and that were developed based on the legal and operational considerations for the situation.

c. **ROE and RUF.** For operations, the responsibility and authority for using military force is generally delegated from the President/SecDef to the supported CCDR/JFC in the form of approved plans/orders with either ROE for operations overseas, or RUF for civil support (CS) within the homeland or while conducting official DOD security functions outside US territory. For a given operation, the ROE/RUF begin at a standard (level) set by the CJCSI 3121.01B, *Standing Rules Of Engagement/Standing Rules For The Use Of Force For US Forces,* or as approved through the chain-of-command in the appropriate plan/order to the supported CCDR. NOTE: ROE/RUF must always be consistent with the inherent right of self defense, but the specifics that determine when and how that right may be exercised may be different for various missions and weapons systems as determined by the responsible commander. Also, when compared to major combat operations, ROE for some smaller-scale operations/actions (i.e., some CT operations) may be more restrictive and detailed, especially in an urban environment, due to national policy concerns for the impact on civilians, their culture, values, and infrastructure. A JFC may begin operations with different ROE/RUF for each type of mission, and especially for CT operations. The JFC responsible for CT should determine early in the planning stage what the required ROE/RUF should be, including anticipating the need for serial changes based on the need for escalation of force, changing phases of an operation, branches/sequels to a plan, etc. Dependent upon the required level of approval for any changes, that JFC must take anticipatory action if the serial changes are to be timely enough for effective operations. When conducting multinational CT operations, the use of military force may be influenced by the differences between US and a HN's and/or a PN's ROE/RUF. Commanders at all levels must take proactive steps to ensure an understanding of ROE by the individual Service member, because a single errant act could cause significant adverse political consequences.

For more detailed discussion on restraint (a joint operations principle) and ROE/RUF, see JP 3-0, Joint Operations.

   d. **Detainee Operations.** CT operations may result in detainees. **Proper handling of detainees is essential not only for possible exploitation purposes, but to prevent violations of the law** (civil or military) and/or national political embarrassment. Of the three categories of detainees, an "enemy combatant" includes a terrorist (properly designated as an "unlawful" enemy combatant). More specifically, for the war on terrorism, the term unlawful enemy combatant includes, but is not limited to, an individual who is, or was part of, or supporting Taliban or al-Qaida forces or associated forces that are engaged in hostilities against the United States or its multinational partners. However, regardless of the detainees' legal status, US forces must treat all detainees humanely and be prepared to properly control, maintain, protect, and account for detainees in accordance with applicable US law, the law of war, and applicable US policy. **Inhumane treatment of detainees is prohibited** by the Uniform Code of Military Justice, domestic and international law, and DOD policy. Accordingly, the stress of combat operations, the need for intelligence, or provocations by captured and/or detained personnel does not justify deviation from this obligation. **The challenges of today's security environment and the nature of the enemy require clear operational and strategic guidance for detainee operations during CT operations.**

For detailed information regarding detainee operations, see JP 3-63, Detainee Operations.

   e. **Domestic Military CT Operations.** Domestic CT operations are considered part of homeland security under the lead of DHS. DHS is considered primary for coordinating Executive Branch efforts to detect, prepare for, prevent, protect against, respond to, and recover from terrorist attacks within the United States. DOJ supports DHS for CT, but also could be the primary Federal agency for some situations. If tasked to support the primary agency for domestic CT operations, DOD would be in a CS role, which would include any support for law enforcement purposes. If a CT situation should formally transcend into a matter of homeland defense (HD), then DOD is the lead for action and interagency coordination for HD.

   (1) SecDef retains the authority to approve use of DOD resources for CS. For CS within the United States, the Joint Staff Joint Director of Military Support must validate requests for assistance, determine what DOD capabilities are available to fulfill the requests, coordinate for the SecDef approval to use DOD assets, and then allocate forces to the combatant command with responsibility for that area of the United States.

   (2) In domestic situations, the Constitution, law, and DOD policy limit the scope and nature of military actions. The President has the authority to direct the use of the

military **against terrorist groups and individuals in the United States** for other than law enforcement actions (i.e., national defense, emergency protection of life and property, and to restore order). The National Guard has a unique role in domestic military operations. Under control of the respective states, National Guard units in Title 32, United States Code (USC) and state active duty status can support a variety of tasks for HD and CS. In its maritime law enforcement role under DHS, the US Coast Guard (USCG), as a Service under DHS, has jurisdiction in both US waters and on the high seas as prescribed in law. Memoranda of agreements between DOD and DHS/USCG exists to facilitate the rapid transfer of forces between DOD and the USCG for support of homeland security, HD, and other defense operations. Therefore, the military response to extraordinary events that requires DOD CS will likely be a coordinated effort between the National Guard (in state active duty or Title 32, USC status), and the Armed Services (Title 10, and Title 14, USC).

(3) Domestic CT activities may involve other civil participants including state, local, and/or tribal governments.

For more information on homeland security, HD, CS, and the coordination of associated interagency activities supporting of those missions, see the National Strategy for Homeland Security, *the* National Response Framework, *the* DOD Strategy for Homeland Defense and Civil Support, *JP 3-27,* Homeland Defense, *and JP 3-28,* Civil Support.

6. Strategic Communication

SC is the focused USG efforts to understand and engage key audiences to create, strengthen, or preserve conditions favorable for the advancement of USG interests, policies, and objectives through the use of coordinated programs, plans, themes, messages, and products synchronized with the actions of all instruments of national power. For CT, SC should focus on understanding the key audiences, building rapport with them, and providing them with timely, user-friendly information that provides a clear understanding of how USG interests, actions, policies, and objectives may be of value to them.

a. **SC Capability.** SC aims to ensure certain audiences have access to information that is easy for them to consume and relevant to decisions they may have to make in regards to the war on terrorism. Information must be accurate and consistent with all actions. Information needs to be developed and presented with the end user in mind. For example, we must understand what is important to the audience in order to share USG interests in context. SC planning and execution should focus capabilities that apply information to create, strengthen, or preserve an information environment favorable to US national interests. **Effective use of SC also can be used to counter VEOs' use of their own form of SC: ideological propaganda and disinformation.** SC planning establishes unity of US themes and messages, emphasizes success, accurately confirms or refutes external reporting on US CT operations, and reinforces the legitimacy of US objectives. Effective use of SC requires extensive interagency coordination.

b. **VEOs Form of SC.** VEOs use the Internet and some mass media for organizational support, intelligence gathering, and offensive actions. Uses of the Internet include command and control, training, dissemination of information and ideology, perception management, and propaganda, as well as open source intelligence gathering. Mass media and other influence networks are used to deliver disinformation and propaganda to further extremist objectives. Extremists are resourceful and adaptive in using IO in support of their own SC strategy to gain and maintain ideological support, fundraise and recruit, and influence key audiences. **Because VEOs are not constrained by truth or accuracy, they can exploit the information environment with considerable effect.**

c. **CT Objectives for DOD SC.** The DOD SC objectives in the war on terrorism are to strengthen the GCTN by supporting PNs, converting moderates to become PNs, weaken sympathy and support for VEOs, provide support for moderate voices, dissuade enablers and supporters of extremists, counter ideological support for terrorism, and deter and disrupt terrorist acts.

d. **CCDR Responsibilities.** CCDRs support the DOD effort as part of the USG effort to develop a more robust SC capability. DOD SC uses the functions of PA, defense support to public diplomacy (DSPD), military diplomacy, and IO and normally within an interagency framework to add synergy to the overall SC effort. CCDRs receive their SC guidance from and coordinate their SC activities with the Office of the Secretary of Defense. Subordinate JFCs must coordinate their SC activities with the CCDR to ensure they are consistent with USG objectives. GCCs must collaborate with the DOS diplomatic missions within their AORs. CCDRs should integrate an SC strategy and incorporate themes, messages, and other relevant factors in their security cooperation plans. During contingency and crisis action planning, CCDRs review SC guidance during mission analysis, and their staffs address SC issues in their staff estimates.

e. **Interaction among SC Elements and Functions.** DOD PA, DSPD, military diplomacy, and IO are synchronized to support SC. However, certain PA, IO, and DSPD activities may be constrained by USG policy or legal considerations. Also, while those capabilities have common interfaces within the information environment, their primary purposes and rules make them separate and distinct. Figure V-2 depicts the general relationships among the elements and functions of SC for CT. While some actions may occur in isolation of others, none should be considered subordinate to another, and it is vital to synchronize the four functions.

7. Information Operations

JP 3-13, *Information Operations*, states, "A key goal of IO is to achieve and maintain information superiority for the US and its allies. Information superiority provides the joint force a competitive advantage only when it is effectively translated into superior decisions." IO are used to create and/or sustain desired and measurable effects on adversary leaders, forces (regular or irregular), information, information systems, and other audiences; while protecting and defending the JFC's own forces actions, information, and information systems. IO are described as the integrated employment of the core capabilities of

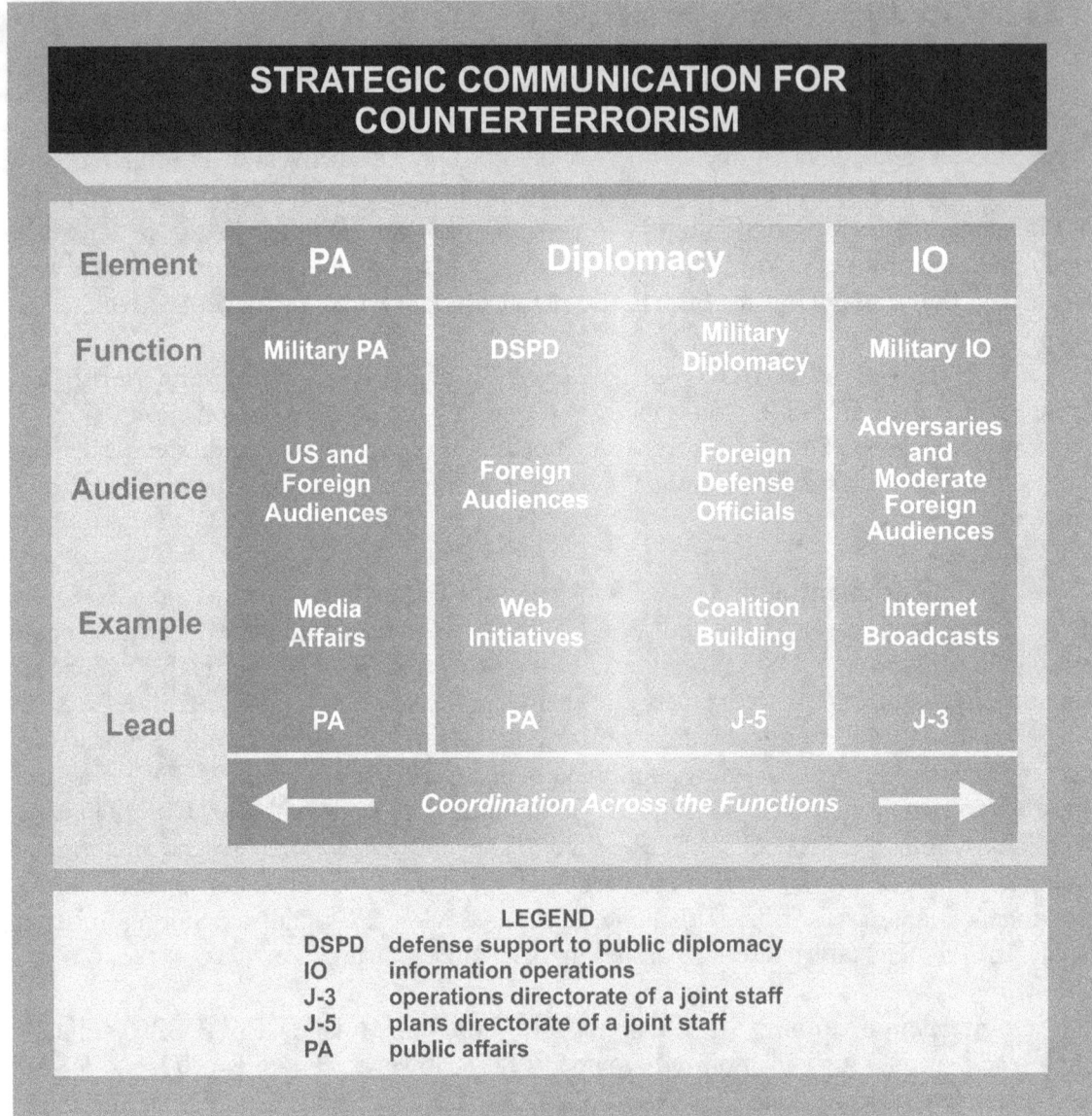

Figure V-2. Strategic Communication for Counterterrorism

electronic warfare, computer network operations, PSYOP, military deception, and operations security, in concert with specified supporting and related capabilities, to influence, disrupt, corrupt or usurp adversarial human and automated decision making while protecting our own. **It is obvious that IO can and should be applied across the breadth and depth of CT operations as a primary means of influencing not only extremists and their supporters, but just as important, the moderates (mainstream populace).**

a. To achieve and maintain information superiority requires a collective effort between the interagency, PNs, and IGOs to include a concerted effort in coordinating and seeking cooperation with NGOs and the private sector in operational areas. Typically, for CT, in addition to intelligence (often limited), it takes effective and efficient use of IO capabilities to gain an operational advantage and exploit or neutralize a terrorist group. CT is a mission area that focuses on effects of operations on people, and in some operational areas the "information war" can determine which side will gain the upper hand in public opinion. A number of terrorist groups have gained sympathy if not support among moderate audiences through disinformation partly based on their IO playing off miscues of the friendly CT forces. An example goal for IO, as it relates to CT, is to help shape public opinion to inhibit recruitment of potential terrorists and their sympathizers, and ultimately create an inhospitable environment for terrorism.

b. In CT operations, a goal is to identify the TAs and use IO to influence the TAs' behavior. Within an operational area there may be a number of TAs and there will likely be multiple synchronized themes, messages, and means of delivery required for each.

(1) CT operations must disrupt terrorists' decision-making capabilities (e.g., information, information processes, C2) that will, in turn, hinder their operating tempo, limit movements across borders, and require increased protective measures to attempt to reduce their vulnerability to attack by United States and PNs forces.

(2) CT operations must disrupt terrorists' IO processes to reduce fear and uncertainty within the United States, its partner and other friendly nations, and other interested parties.

(3) The intent of CT operations as they relate to IO is to shape and influence the terrorists' informational environment. CT operations must use all available tools to compel the TA to do or not do a certain action.

c. A JFC's IO program will be linked through the CCDR to USG SC.

For more detailed discussion of IO, refer to JP 3-13, Information Operations.

Intentionally Blank

APPENDIX A
REFERENCES

The development of JP 3-26 is based upon the following primary references:

1. **General**

    a. *Unified Command Plan.*

    b. *Irregular Warfare Joint Operating Concept.*

    c. *National Security Strategy of the United States of America.*

    d. *National Strategy for Combating Terrorism.*

    e. *Quadrennial Defense Review Report*, Department of Defense.

    f. *National Military Strategic Plan for the War on Terrorism.*

    g. USSOCOM Concept Plan 7500, *Department of Defense Global War on Terrorism Campaign Plan* (classified).

    h. USSOCOM Publication 3-33, *Conventional Forces and Special Operations Forces Integration and Interoperability Handbook and Checklist* (Version 2).

2. **Chairman of the Joint Chiefs of Staff**

    a. CJCSI 3110.03, *Logistics Supplement To The Joint Strategies Capabilities Plan (JSCP).*

    b. CJCSI 3121.01B, *Standing Rules of Engagement/Standing Rules for the Use of Force for US Forces.*

    c. CJCSI 5120.02A, *Joint Doctrine Development System.*

    d. CJCSI 5810.01C, *Implementation of the DOD Law of War Program.*

    e. JP 1, *Doctrine for the Armed Forces of the United States.*

    f. JP 1-02, *Department of Defense Dictionary of Military and Associated Terms.*

    g. JP 1-04, *Legal Support to Military Operations.*

    h. JP 2-0, *Joint Intelligence.*

i. JP 2-01, *Joint and National Intelligence Support to Military Operations.*

j. JP 3-0, *Joint Operations.*

k. JP 3-05, *Doctrine for Joint Special Operations.*

l. JP 3-05.1, *Joint Special Operations Task Force Operations.*

m. JP 3-07.2, *Antiterrorism.*

n. JP 3-08, *Interorganizational Coordination During Joint Operations,* Vol. I & II.

o. JP 3-10, *Joint Security Operations in Theater.*

p. JP 3-13, *Information Operations.*

q. JP 3-13.2, *Psychological Operations.*

r. JP 3-16, *Multinational Operations.*

s. JP 3-22, *Foreign Internal Defense (FID).*

t. JP 3-24, *Counterinsurgency Operations.*

u. JP 3-27, *Homeland Defense.*

v. JP 3-28, *Civil Support.*

w. JP 3-30, *Command and Control for Joint Air Operations.*

x. JP 3-33, *Joint Task Force Headquarters.*

y. JP 3-40, *Combating Weapons of Mass Destruction.*

z. JP 3-57, *Civil-Military Operations.*

aa. JP 3-60, *Joint Targeting.*

bb. JP 3-63, *Detainee Operations.*

cc. JP 4-0, *Joint Logistics.*

dd. JP 5-0, *Joint Operation Planning.*

ee. JP 6-0, *Joint Communications System.*

3. Service Documents

US Army Training and Doctrine Command, *A Military Guide to Terrorism in the Twenty-First Century*, 15 August 2005 (Version 3.0).

4. Acknowledgements

The following are acknowledged for their specific contributions to the content of the US Army Training and Doctrine Command, *A Military Guide to Terrorism in the Twenty-First Century*, 15 August 2005 (Version 3.0), which was used extensively for portions of Chapter II, "Terrorist Threats."

a. John Arquilla and David Ronfeldt, ed., *Networks and Netwars* (Santa Monica: RAND, 2001), 9.

b. Peter Chalk, "Threats to the Maritime Environment: Piracy and Terrorism," (RAND Stakeholder Consultation, Ispra, Italy 28-30 October 2002): 9.

c. Martha Crenshaw, "Suicide Terrorism in Comparative Perspective," in *Countering Suicide Terrorism* (Herzilya, Israel: The International Policy Institute for Counter Terrorism, The Interdisciplinary Center, 2002), 21.

d. Lou Dolinar, "Cell Phones Jury-rigged to Detonate Bombs," *Newsday.com*, 15 March 2004; available from http://www.newsday.com/news/nationworld/ny-wocell153708827mar15,0,1644248.story?coll=ny-nationworldheadlines; Internet; accessed 15 March 2004.

e. Rachael Ehrenfeld, *IRA + PLO + Terror* [journal on-line] American Center for Democracy (ACD), 21 August 2002; available from http://public-integrity.org/publications21.htm; Internet; accessed 13 February 2004.

f. Christopher C. Harmon, *Terrorism Today* (London: Frank Cass Publishers, 2000; reprint, Portland: Frank Cass Publishers, 2001), 198.

g. Seth Hettena, "Earth Liberation Front Claims Responsibility for San Diego Arson," *The Mercury News*, 18 August 2003; available from http://www.mercurynews.com/mld/mercurynews/news/local/6562462.htm; Internet; accessed 17 March 2004. http://www.iseas.edu.sg/viewpoint/ggosep03.pdf; Internet; accessed 2 April 2004.

h. Bruce Hoffman, *Inside Terrorism* (New York: Columbia University Press, 1998).

i. David E. Long, *The Anatomy of Terrorism* (New York: THE FREE PRESS, A Division of Macmillan, Inc., 1990).

j. John McWethy et al., no title, *ABCNews.Com,* 18 October 2000; available from http://www.abcnews.go.com/sections/world/ DailyNews/cole001018b.html; Internet; accessed 9 January 2003.

k. Bob Newman, "Terrorists Feared to Be Planning Sub-Surface Naval Attacks," *CNS News.com,* 3 December 2002; available from http://www.cnsnews.com/Foreign Bureaus/ archive/200212/FOR20021203a.html; Internet; accessed 19 March 2004.

l. Graham Gerard Ong, "Next Stop, Maritime Terrorism," *Viewpoints* (12 September 2003): 1; available from R Michael Richardson, "A Time Bomb for Global Trade: Maritime-related Terrorism in an Age of Weapons of Mass Destruction," *Viewpoints* (25 February 2004): 8; available from http://www.iseas.edu.sg/viewpoint/mricsumfeb04.pdf; Internet; accessed 5 April 2004.

m. Walter Reich, ed., *Origins of Terrorism: Psychologies, Ideologies, Theologies, States of Mind*, rev. ed. (Washington: Woodrow Wilson Center Press, 1998).

n. Jan Schuurman, *Tourists or Terrorists?* [press review on-line] Radio Netherlands, 25 April 2002; available from http://www.rnw.nl/hotspots/html/irel020425.html; Internet; accessed 13 February 2004.

o. Yoram Schweitzer, "Suicide Terrorism: Development and Main Characteristics," in *Countering Suicide.*

p. Don Thompson, "British Ecoterror Tactics Spread to US Activists," *The Mercury News*, 10 May 2003, 1-2; available from http://www.mercurynews.com/mld/ mercurynews/news/local/5832723.htm?1c; Internet; accessed 21 April 2004.

q. Ben N. Venzke, *al Qaeda Targeting Guidance* - Version 1.0 (Alexandria, VA: IntelCenter/Tempest Publishing, LLC, 2004).

r. Ben Venzke and Aimee Ibrahim, *The al-Qaeda Threat, An Analytical Guide to al-Qaeda's Tactics & Targets* (Alexandria: Tempest Publishing, 2003).

s. "Saboteurs Disable Critical Iraqi Oil Pipeline," *HoustonChronicle.com*, 8 September 2003; available from http://www.chron.com/cs/CDA/ssistory.mpl/ special/iraq/2087438; Internet; accessed 16 January 2004.

t. "Terrorists Demand Extortion Cash in Euros," *TCM Breaking News* (4 September 2001): 1; available from http://archives.tcm.ie/breakingnews/2001/09/04/story22584.asp; Internet; accessed 31 March 2004.

u. *Encyclopedia of World Terror*, 1997 ed., s.v. "Bombing." 277 Department of Justice, Federal Bureau of Investigation, Counterterrorism Division, Terrorism 2000/2001, Report 0308, (Washington, D.C., 2004).

v. *Terrorism* (Herzilya, Israel: The International Policy Institute for Counter Terrorism, The Interdisciplinary Center, 2002), 85. 306 Ehud Sprinzak, "Rational Fanatics," *Foreign Policy,* no. 120 (September/October 2000).

Intentionally Blank

APPENDIX B
ADMINISTRATIVE INSTRUCTIONS

1. User Comments

Users in the field are highly encouraged to submit comments on this publication to: Commander, United States Joint Forces Command, Joint Warfighting Center, ATTN: Doctrine and Education Group, 116 Lake View Parkway, Suffolk, VA 23435-2697. These comments should address content (accuracy, usefulness, consistency, and organization), writing, and appearance.

2. Authorship

The lead agent for this publication is the United States Special Operations Command (SOKF-J7). The Joint Staff doctrine sponsor for this publication is the Directorate for Strategic Plans and Policy (J-5).

3. Change Recommendations

a. Recommendations for urgent changes to this publication should be submitted:

TO: CDRUSSOCOM MACDILL AFB FL//SOKF-J7-DD//
INFO: JOINT STAFF WASHINGTON DC//J3/J7-JEDD//
        CDRUSJFCOM SUFFOLK VA//JT10//

Routine changes should be submitted electronically to Commander, Joint Warfighting Center, Doctrine and Education Group and info the Lead Agent and the Director for Operational Plans and Joint Force Development J-7/JEDD via the CJCS JEL at http://www.dtic.mil/doctrine.

b. When a Joint Staff directorate submits a proposal to the Chairman of the Joint Chiefs of Staff that would change source document information reflected in this publication, that directorate will include a proposed change to this publication as an enclosure to its proposal. The Military Services and other organizations are requested to notify the Joint Staff J-7 when changes to source documents reflected in this publication are initiated.

c. Record of Changes:

CHANGE NUMBER	COPY NUMBER	DATE OF CHANGE	DATE ENTERED	POSTED BY	REMARKS

4.   Distribution of Publications

Local reproduction is authorized and access to unclassified publications is unrestricted. However, access to and reproduction authorization for classified joint publications must be in accordance with DOD 5200.1-R, *Information Security Program.*

5.   Distribution of Electronic Publications

a. Joint Staff J-7 will not print copies of JPs for distribution. Electronic versions are available on JDEIS at https://jdeis.js.mil (NIPRNET), and https://jdeis.js.smil.mil (SIPRNET) and on the JEL at http://www.dtic.mil/doctrine (NIPRNET).

b. Only approved joint publications and joint test publications are releasable outside the combatant commands, Services, and Joint Staff. Release of any classified joint publication to foreign governments or foreign nationals must be requested through the local embassy (Defense Attaché Office) to DIA Foreign Liaison Office, PO-FL, Room 1E811, 7400 Pentagon, Washington, DC 20301-7400.

c. CD-ROM. Upon request of a JDDC member, the Joint Staff J-7 will produce and deliver one CD-ROM with current joint publications.

GLOSSARY
PART I — ABBREVIATIONS AND ACRONYMS

A&P	analysis and production
ACSA	acquisition and cross-servicing agreement
AO	area of operations
AOR	area of responsibility
APOD	aerial port of debarkation
APOE	aerial port of embarkation
C2	command and control
CA	civil affairs
CAO	civil affairs operations
CBRN	chemical, biological, radiological, and nuclear
CbT	combating terrorism
CCDR	combatant commander
CDRJSOTF	commander, joint special operations task force
CDRUSNORTHCOM	Commander, United States Northern Command
CDRUSSOCOM	Commander, United States Special Operations Command
CF	conventional forces
CJCS	Chairman of the Joint Chiefs of Staff
CJCSI	Chairman of the Joint Chiefs of Staff instruction
CJTF	commander, joint task force
CM	consequence management
CMO	civil-military operations
COA	course of action
COCOM	combatant command (command authority)
COG	center of gravity
COIN	counterinsurgency
CONOPS	concept of operations
CS	civil support
CSA	combat support agency
CSO	Center for Special Operations (USSOCOM)
CSS	combat service support
CT	counterterrorism
CTAF	counterterrorism analytical framework
DAFL	directive authority for logistics
DHS	Department of Homeland Security
DIOCC	Defense Intelligence Operations Coordination Center
DNI	Director of National Intelligence
DOD	Department of Defense
DOJ	Department of Justice
DOS	Department of State

DSPD	defense support to public diplomacy
DTA	dynamic threat assessment
FBI	Federal Bureau of Investigation
FID	foreign internal defense
FSF	foreign security forces
GCC	geographic combatant commander
GCTN	global combating terrorism network
GEF	Guidance for Employment of the Force
GWOT	global war on terrorism
HD	homeland defense
HN	host nation
HNS	host-nation support
HSC	Homeland Security Council
HVI	high-value individual
IC	intelligence community
IED	improvised explosive device
IGO	intergovernmental organization
IO	information operations
IRA	Provisional Irish Republican Army
ISB	intermediate staging base
ISR	intelligence, surveillance, and reconnaissance
ITL	intelligence task list
IW	irregular warfare
J-4	logistics directorate of a joint staff
JAOC	joint air operations center
JDDOC	joint deployment and distribution operations center
JFACC	joint force air component commander
JFC	joint force commander
JFCC-ISR	Joint Functional Component Command for Intelligence, Surveillance, and Reconnaissance
JIACG	joint interagency coordination group
JITF-CT	Joint Intelligence Task Force for Combating Terrorism
JOA	joint operations area
JP	joint publication
JSCP	Joint Strategic Capabilities Plan
JSOA	joint special operations area
JSOTF	joint special operations task force
JTF	joint task force
LOC	line of communications
LOO	line of operations

NCTC	National Counterterrorism Center
NGO	nongovernmental organization
NISP	national intelligence support plan
NMSP-WOT	National Military Strategic Plan for the War on Terrorism
NORAD	North American Aerospace Defense Command
NSC	National Security Council
OGA	other government agency
OPCON	operational control
OPE	operational preparation of the environment
PA	public affairs
PN	partner nation
PSYOP	psychological operations
ROE	rules of engagement
RUF	rules for the use of force
SC	strategic communication
SecDef	Secretary of Defense
SFA	security force assistance
SO	special operations
SOF	special operations forces
SPOD	seaport of debarkation
TA	target audience
TACON	tactical control
TSOC	theater special operations command
UAS	unmanned aircraft system
UNSCR	United Nations Security Council resolution
USC	United States Code
USCG	United States Coast Guard
USG	United States Government
USNORTHCOM	United States Northern Command
USSOCOM	United States Special Operations Command
USSTRATCOM	United States Strategic Command
UW	unconventional warfare
VEO	violent extremist organization
WMD	weapons of mass destruction

Unless otherwise annotated, this publication is the proponent for all terms and definitions found in the glossary. Upon approval, JP 1-02, *Department of Defense Dictionary of Military and Associated Terms*, will reflect this publication as the source document for these terms and definitions.

acquisition and cross-servicing agreement. Agreements negotiated on a bilateral basis with US allies or coalition partners that allow US forces to exchange most common types of support, including food, fuel, transportation, ammunition, and equipment. Authority to negotiate these agreements is usually delegated to the combatant commander by the Secretary of Defense. Authority to execute these agreements lies with the Secretary of Defense, and may or may not be delegated. Governed by legal guidelines, these agreements are used for contingencies, peacekeeping operations, unforeseen emergencies, or exercises to correct logistic deficiencies that cannot be adequately corrected by national means. The support received or given is reimbursed under the conditions of the acquisition and cross-servicing agreement. Also called ACSA. (JP 1-02. SOURCE: JP 4-08)

alliance. The relationship that results from a formal agreement (e.g., treaty) between two or more nations for broad, long-term objectives that further the common interests of the members. (JP 1-02. SOURCE: JP 3-0)

antiterrorism. Defensive measures used to reduce the vulnerability of individuals and property to terrorist acts, to include limited response and containment by local military and civilian forces. Also called AT. (JP 1-02. SOURCE: JP 3-07.2)

campaign. A series of related major operations aimed at achieving strategic and operational objectives within a given time and space. (JP 1-02. SOURCE: JP 5-0)

campaign plan. A joint operation plan for a series of related major operations aimed at achieving strategic or operational objectives within a given time and space. (JP 1-02. SOURCE: JP 5-0)

center of gravity. The source of power that provides moral or physical strength, freedom of action, or will to act. Also called COG. (JP 1-02. SOURCE: JP 3-0)

civil affairs. Designated Active and Reserve Component forces and units organized, trained, and equipped specifically to conduct civil affairs operations and to support civil-military operations. Also called CA. (JP 1-02. SOURCE: JP 3-57)

civil affairs operations. Those military operations conducted by civil affairs forces that (1) enhance the relationship between military forces and civil authorities in localities where military forces are present; (2) require coordination with other interagency organizations, intergovernmental organizations, nongovernmental organizations, indigenous populations and institutions, and the private sector; and (3) involve application of functional specialty skills that normally are the responsibility of civil government to enhance the conduct of civil-military operations. Also called CAO. (JP 1-02. SOURCE: JP 3-57)

civil-military operations. The activities of a commander that establish, maintain, influence, or exploit relations between military forces, governmental and nongovernmental civilian organizations and authorities, and the civilian populace in a friendly, neutral, or hostile operational area in order to facilitate military operations, to consolidate and achieve operational US objectives. Civil-military operations may include performance by military forces of activities and functions normally the responsibility of the local, regional, or national government. These activities may occur prior to, during, or subsequent to other military actions. They may also occur, if directed, in the absence of other military operations. Civil-military operations may be performed by designated civil affairs, by other military forces, or by a combination of civil affairs and other forces. Also called CMO. (JP 1-02. SOURCE: JP 3-57)

coalition. An ad hoc arrangement between two or more nations for common action. (JP 1-02. SOURCE: JP 5-0)

combating terrorism. Actions, including antiterrorism and counterterrorism, taken to oppose terrorism throughout the entire threat spectrum. Also called CbT. (This term and its definition modify the existing term and its definition and are approved for inclusion in JP 1-02.)

consequence management. Actions taken to maintain or restore essential services and manage and mitigate problems resulting from disasters and catastrophes, including natural, man-made, or terrorist incidents. Also called CM. (JP 1-02. SOURCE: JP 3-28)

conventional forces. 1. Those forces capable of conducting operations using nonnuclear weapons. 2. Those forces other than designated special operations forces. (JP 1-02. SOURCE: JP 3-05)

coordinating authority. A commander or individual assigned responsibility for coordinating specific functions or activities involving forces of two or more Military Departments, two or more joint force components, or two or more forces of the same Service. The commander or individual has the authority to require consultation between the agencies involved, but does not have the authority to compel agreement. In the event that essential agreement cannot be obtained, the matter shall be referred to the appointing authority. Coordinating authority is a consultation relationship, not an authority through which command may be exercised. Coordinating authority is more applicable to planning and similar activities than to operations. (JP 1-02. SOURCE: JP 1)

counterinsurgency. Comprehensive civilian and military efforts taken to simultaneously defeat and contain an insurgency and to address any core grievances. Also called COIN. (JP 1-02. SOURCE: JP 3-24)

counterterrorism. Actions taken directly against terrorist networks and indirectly to influence and render global and regional environments inhospitable to terrorist networks. Also called CT. (This term and its definition modify the existing term and its definition and are approved for inclusion in JP 1-02.)

critical capability. A means that is considered a crucial enabler for a center of gravity to function as such and is essential to the accomplishment of the specified or assumed objective(s). (JP 1-02. SOURCE: JP 5-0)

critical requirement. An essential condition, resource, and means for a critical capability to be fully operational. (JP 1-02. SOURCE: JP 5-0)

critical vulnerability. An aspect of a critical requirement which is deficient or vulnerable to direct or indirect attack that will create decisive or significant effects. (JP 1-02. SOURCE: JP 5-0)

defense support to public diplomacy. Those activities and measures taken by the Department of Defense components to support and facilitate public diplomacy efforts of the United States Government. Also called DSPD. (JP 1-02. SOURCE: JP 3-13)

direct action. Short-duration strikes and other small-scale offensive actions conducted as a special operation in hostile, denied, or politically sensitive environments and which employ specialized military capabilities to seize, destroy, capture, exploit, recover, or damage designated targets. Direct action differs from conventional offensive actions in the level of physical and political risk, operational techniques, and the degree of discriminate and precise use of force to achieve specific objectives. Also called DA. (JP 1-02. SOURCE: JP 3-05)

foreign internal defense. Participation by civilian and military agencies of a government in any of the action programs taken by another government or other designated organization to free and protect its society from subversion, lawlessness, and insurgency. Also called FID. (JP 1-02. SOURCE: JP 3-22)

homeland. The physical region that includes the continental United States, Alaska, Hawaii, United States possessions and territories, and surrounding territorial waters and airspace. (JP 1-02. SOURCE: JP 3-28)

homeland defense. The protection of United States sovereignty, territory, domestic population, and critical defense infrastructure against external threats and aggression or other threats as directed by the President. Also called HD. (JP 1-02. SOURCE: JP 3-27)

homeland security. A concerted national effort to prevent terrorist attacks within the United States; reduce America's vulnerability to terrorism, major disasters, and other emergencies; and minimize the damage and recover from attacks, major disasters, and other emergencies that occur. Also called HS. (JP 1-02. SOURCE: JP 3-28)

information operations. The integrated employment of the core capabilities of electronic warfare, computer network operations, psychological operations, military deception, and operations security, in concert with specified supporting and related capabilities, to influence, disrupt, corrupt or usurp adversarial human and automated decision making while protecting our own. Also called IO. (JP 1-02. SOURCE: JP 3-13)

insurgency. The organized use of subversion and violence by a group or movement that seeks to overthrow or force change of a governing authority. Insurgency can also refer to the group itself. (JP 1-02. SOURCE: JP 3-24)

irregular warfare. A violent struggle among state and non-state actors for legitimacy and influence over the relevant population(s). Irregular warfare favors indirect and asymmetric approaches, though it may employ the full range of military and other capacities, in order to erode an adversary's power, influence, and will. Also called IW. (JP 1-02. SOURCE: JP 1)

joint interagency coordination group. An interagency staff group that establishes regular, timely, and collaborative working relationships between civilian and military operational planners. Composed of US Government civilian and military experts accredited to the combatant commander and tailored to meet the requirements of a supported joint force commander, the joint interagency coordination group provides the joint force commander with the capability to coordinate with other US Government civilian agencies and departments. Also called JIACG. (JP 1-02. SOURCE: JP 3-08)

joint special operations area. An area of land, sea, and airspace assigned by a joint force commander to the commander of a joint special operations force to conduct special operations activities. It may be limited in size to accommodate a discrete direct action mission or may be extensive enough to allow a continuing broad range of unconventional warfare operations. Also called JSOA. (JP 1-02. SOURCE: JP 3-0)

joint special operations task force. A joint task force composed of special operations units from more than one Service, formed to carry out a specific special operation or prosecute special operations in support of a theater campaign or other operations. The joint special operations task force may have conventional non-special operations units assigned or attached to support the conduct of specific missions. Also called JSOTF. (JP 1-02. SOURCE: JP 3-05)

joint task force. A joint force that is constituted and so designated by the Secretary of Defense, a combatant commander, a subunified commander, or an existing joint task force commander. Also called JTF. (JP 1-02. SOURCE: JP 1)

line of operations. 1. A logical line that connects actions on nodes and/or decisive points related in time and purpose with an objective(s). 2. A physical line that defines the interior or exterior orientation of the force in relation to the enemy or that connects actions on nodes and/or decisive points related in time and space to an objective(s). Also called LOO. (JP 1-02. SOURCE: JP 3-0)

multinational. Between two or more forces or agencies of two or more nations or coalition partners. See also coalition. (JP 1-02. SOURCE: JP 5-0)

multinational force. A force composed of military elements of nations who have formed an alliance or coalition for some specific purpose. Also called MNF. (JP 1-02. SOURCE: JP 1)

nongovernmental organization. A private, self-governing, not-for-profit organization dedicated to alleviating human suffering; and/or promoting education, health care, economic development, environmental protection, human rights, and conflict resolution; and/or encouraging the establishment of democratic institutions and civil society. Also called NGO. (JP 1-02. SOURCE: 3-08)

operational art. The application of creative imagination by commanders and staffs — supported by their skill, knowledge, and experience — to design strategies, campaigns, and major operations and organize and employ military forces. Operational art integrates ends, ways, and means across the levels of war. (JP 1-02. SOURCE: JP 3-0)

operational design. The conception and construction of the framework that underpins a campaign or major operation plan and its subsequent execution. (JP 1-02. SOURCE: JP 3-0)

operational environment. A composite of the conditions, circumstances, and influences that affect the employment of capabilities and bear on the decisions of the commander. Also called OE. (JP 1-02. SOURCE: JP 3-0)

psychological operations. Planned operations to convey selected information and indicators to foreign audiences to influence their emotions, motives, objective reasoning, and ultimately the behavior of foreign governments, organizations, groups, and individuals. The purpose of psychological operations is to induce or reinforce foreign attitudes and behavior favorable to the originator's objectives. Also called PSYOP. (JP 1-02. SOURCE: JP 3-13.2)

public affairs. Those public information, command information, and community relations activities directed toward both the external and internal publics with interest in the Department of Defense. Also called PA. (JP 1-02. SOURCE: JP 3-61)

raid. An operation to temporarily seize an area in order to secure information, confuse an adversary, capture personnel or equipment, or to destroy a capability. It ends with a planned withdrawal upon completion of the assigned mission. (JP 1-02. SOURCE: JP 3-0)

rules for the use of force. Directives issued to guide United States forces on the use of force during various operations. These directives may take the form of execute orders, deployment orders, memoranda of agreement, or plans. Also called RUF. (JP 1-02. SOURCE: JP 3-28)

rules of engagement. Directives issued by competent military authority that delineate the circumstances and limitations under which United States forces will initiate and/or continue combat engagement with other forces encountered. Also called ROE. (JP 1-02. SOURCE: JP 1-04)

security cooperation. All Department of Defense interactions with foreign defense establishments to build defense relationships that promote specific US security interests, develop allied and friendly military capabilities for self-defense and multinational operations, and provide US forces with peacetime and contingency access to a host nation. (JP 1-02. SOURCE: JP 3-07.1)

special operations. Operations conducted in hostile, denied, or politically sensitive environments to achieve military, diplomatic, informational, and/or economic objectives employing military capabilities for which there is no broad conventional force requirement. These operations often require covert, clandestine, or low visibility capabilities. Special operations are applicable across the range of military operations. They can be conducted independently or in conjunction with operations of conventional forces or other government agencies and may include operations through, with, or by indigenous or surrogate forces. Special operations differ from conventional operations in degree of physical and political risk, operational techniques, mode of employment, independence from friendly support, and dependence on detailed operational intelligence and indigenous assets. Also called SO. (JP 1-02. SOURCE: JP 3-05)

special operations forces. Those Active and Reserve Component forces of the Military Services designated by the Secretary of Defense and specifically organized, trained, and equipped to conduct and support special operations. Also called SOF. (JP 1-02. SOURCE: JP 3-05.1)

stability operations. An overarching term encompassing various military missions, tasks, and activities conducted outside the United States in coordination with other instruments of national power to maintain or reestablish a safe and secure environment, provide essential governmental services, emergency infrastructure reconstruction, and humanitarian relief. (JP 1-02. SOURCE: JP 3-0)

strategic communication. Focused United States Government efforts to understand and engage key audiences to create, strengthen, or preserve conditions favorable for the advancement of United States Government interests, policies, and objectives through the use of coordinated programs, plans, themes, messages, and products synchronized with the actions of all instruments of national power. (JP 1-02. SOURCE: JP 5-0)

targeting. The process of selecting and prioritizing targets and matching the appropriate response to them, considering operational requirements and capabilities. (JP 1-02. SOURCE: JP 3-0)

terrorism. The calculated use of unlawful violence or threat of unlawful violence to inculcate fear; intended to coerce or to intimidate governments or societies in the pursuit of goals that are generally political, religious, or ideological. (JP 1-02. SOURCE: JP 3-07.2)

terrorist. An individual who commits an act or acts of violence or threatens violence in pursuit of political, religious, or ideological objectives. (JP 1-02. SOURCE: JP 3-07.2)

terrorist group. Any number of terrorists who assemble together, have a unifying relationship, or are organized for the purpose of committing an act or acts of violence or threatens violence in pursuit of their political, religious, or ideological objectives. (JP 1-02. SOURCE: JP 3-07.2)

theater special operations command. A subordinate unified or other joint command established by a joint force commander to plan, coordinate, conduct, and support joint special operations within the joint force commander's assigned operational area. Also called TSOC. (JP 1-02. SOURCE: JP 3-05.1)

time-sensitive target. A joint force commander designated target requiring immediate response because it is a highly lucrative, fleeting target of opportunity or it poses (or will soon pose) a danger to friendly forces. Also called TST. (JP 1-02. SOURCE: JP 3-60)

transnational threat. Any activity, individual, or group not tied to a particular country or region that operates across international boundaries and threatens United States national security or interests. (Approved for inclusion in JP 1-02.)

unified action. The synchronization, coordination, and/or integration of the activities of governmental and nongovernmental entities with military operations to achieve unity of effort. (JP 1-02. SOURCE: JP 1)

weapons of mass destruction. Chemical, biological, radiological, or nuclear weapons capable of a high order of destruction or causing mass casualties and exclude the means of transporting or propelling the weapon where such means is a separable and divisible part from the weapon. Also called WMD. (JP 1-02. SOURCE: JP 3-40)

JOINT DOCTRINE PUBLICATIONS HIERARCHY

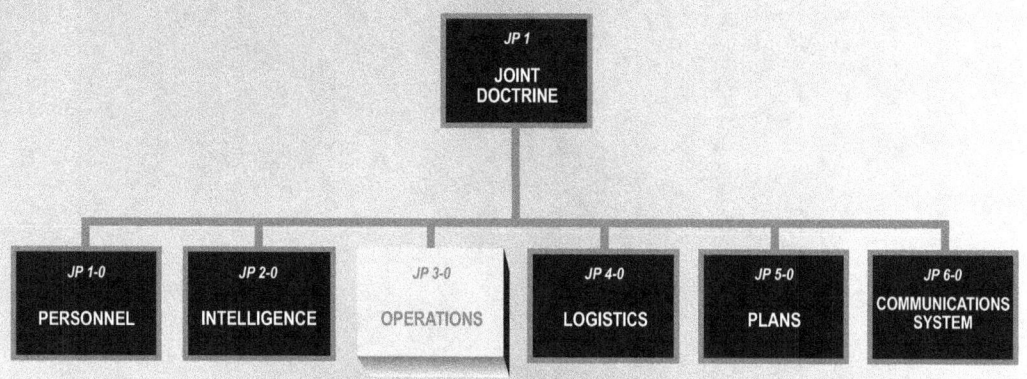

All joint publications are organized into a comprehensive hierarchy as shown in the chart above. **Joint Publication (JP) 3-26** is in the **Operations** series of joint doctrine publications. The diagram below illustrates an overview of the development process:

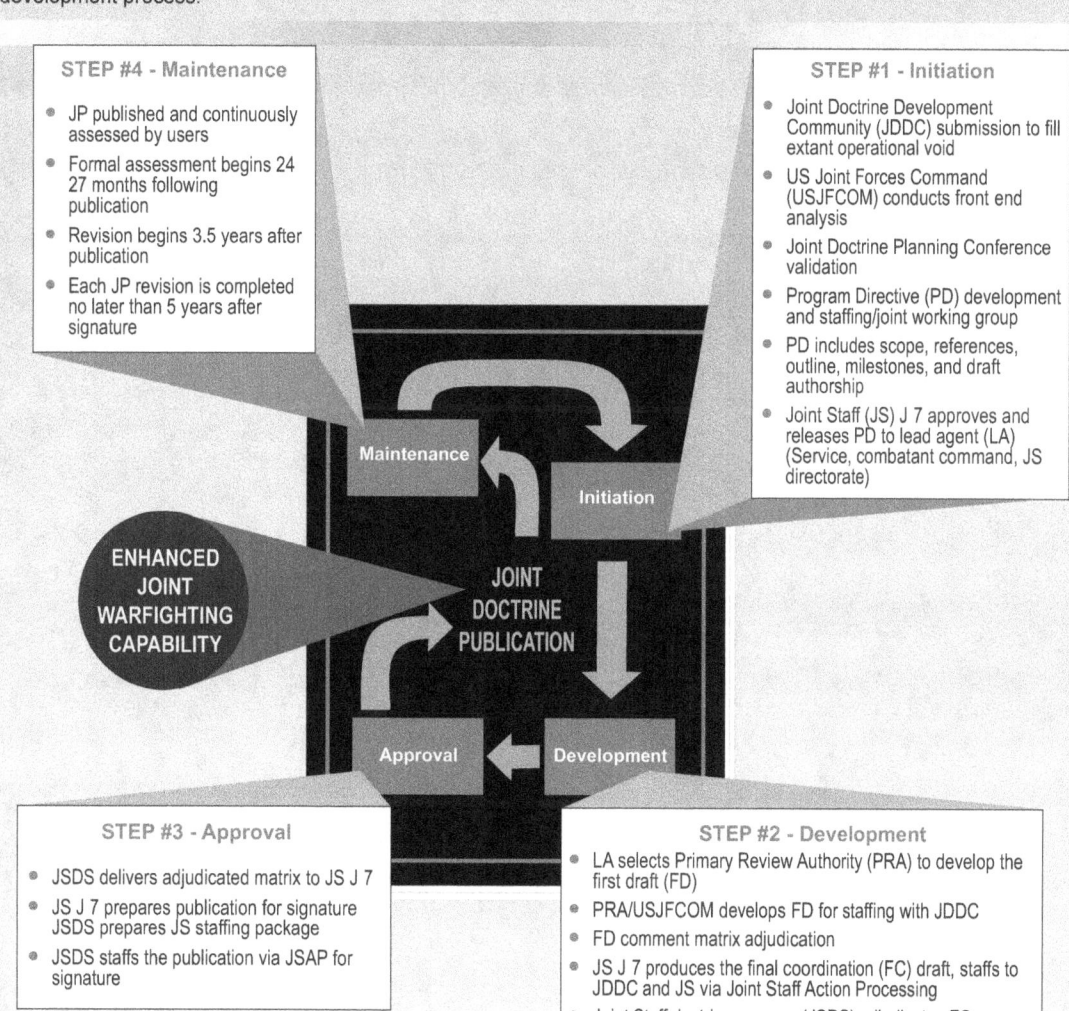

STEP #4 - Maintenance

- JP published and continuously assessed by users
- Formal assessment begins 24 27 months following publication
- Revision begins 3.5 years after publication
- Each JP revision is completed no later than 5 years after signature

STEP #1 - Initiation

- Joint Doctrine Development Community (JDDC) submission to fill extant operational void
- US Joint Forces Command (USJFCOM) conducts front end analysis
- Joint Doctrine Planning Conference validation
- Program Directive (PD) development and staffing/joint working group
- PD includes scope, references, outline, milestones, and draft authorship
- Joint Staff (JS) J 7 approves and releases PD to lead agent (LA) (Service, combatant command, JS directorate)

STEP #3 - Approval

- JSDS delivers adjudicated matrix to JS J 7
- JS J 7 prepares publication for signature JSDS prepares JS staffing package
- JSDS staffs the publication via JSAP for signature

STEP #2 - Development

- LA selects Primary Review Authority (PRA) to develop the first draft (FD)
- PRA/USJFCOM develops FD for staffing with JDDC
- FD comment matrix adjudication
- JS J 7 produces the final coordination (FC) draft, staffs to JDDC and JS via Joint Staff Action Processing
- Joint Staff doctrine sponsor (JSDS) adjudicates FC comment matrix
- FC Joint working group